I0020037

App Development

App Programming and Development for Beginners

(The Quick Way to Learn App Development and Blogging)

Dustin Hodges

Published By **Ryan Princeton**

Dustin Hodges

All Rights Reserved

App Development: App Programming and Development for Beginners (The Quick Way to Learn App Development and Blogging)

ISBN 978-1-77485-873-8

No part of this guidebook shall be reproduced in any form without permission in writing from the publisher except in the case of brief quotations embodied in critical articles or reviews.

Legal & Disclaimer

The information contained in this ebook is not designed to replace or take the place of any form of medicine or professional medical advice. The information in this ebook has been provided for educational & entertainment purposes only.

The information contained in this book has been compiled from sources deemed reliable, and it is accurate to the best of the Author's knowledge; however, the Author cannot guarantee its accuracy and validity and cannot be held liable for any errors or omissions. Changes are periodically made to this book. You must consult your doctor or get professional medical advice before using any of the suggested remedies, techniques, or information in this book.

Upon using the information contained in this book, you agree to hold harmless the Author from and against any damages, costs, and expenses, including any legal fees potentially resulting from the application of any of the information provided by this guide. This disclaimer applies to any damages or injury caused by the use and application, whether directly or indirectly, of any advice or information presented, whether for breach of contract, tort, negligence, personal injury, criminal intent, or under any other cause of action.

You agree to accept all risks of using the information presented inside this book. You need to consult a professional medical practitioner in order to ensure you are both able and healthy enough to participate in this program.

TABLE OF CONTENTS

Chapter 1: The Way To Total 'Appyness

"A journey of one thousand miles

It all starts with a single step."

--Lao Tzu

In the direction of total happiness, we'll take you on a step-by- process journey to create your debut Android app. We will look at the beginning steps of coming up with concepts, before launch your app in Google Play Store. Google Play Store, along with easy ways to promote your app.

If you've never made your own Android application prior to now, don't worry We'll go through this journey with you. Each step is broken into. By the end of the book, you'll be able launch your own Android application in less than 30 minutes. You don't require any special computer skills, however, you'll have to make the first step and remain focused.

When you've finished reading this book, make sure to follow the steps you learn as you go, and then take the book off and experiment with what's being described. If you practice the concepts you've learned as you go You will be more prepared to create more complicated apps in the next few months.

Tools for trade

For you to start it is necessary to be able to use certain tools that you can use to build your Android application. It's not necessary to have a lot of tools to begin creating your first app, and you don't have to spend any money to create your app.

Internet Access. The main tool we'll use to build the app is cloud-based. This means that it's accessible online, and you'll require an internet connection for it to work. The good thing is that you can connect to it by using wifi from a laptop/computer or connect to it using your tablet or mobile phone. If you want to choose but it's much simpler to use a laptop/computer since the viewing space is larger.

Appyet. The application we'll be using to build our application is Appyet.com. You'll need to sign up for an account for free through www.appyet.com. When you first log on to Appyet it is necessary to click at in the upper right "Sign for an account, " and you will be asked to provide four pieces of data: email and password, as well as your first and the last. Start now to create your account.

Image editing software for image editing. It is possible to make use of an image editor software for free included in your laptop. For example, on Microsoft Windows, that is "Paint"; there are others available--for example, Paintshop Pro - http://www.paintshoppro.com/en/free-trials/ (Free 30 day trial) or GIMP https://www.gimp.org/

If you want, you can buy more advanced image editing software such as Adobe Photoshop.

An Android Device. While you are able to create your application without having using an Android device being around, having one can be useful when testing. You can use an emulator to do this; it is, however, slightly more complicated--find out more at http://developer.android.com

If you keep reading the article, we will explain all that you require to learn about how to make use of Appyet.

IDEAS CREATION

We'll spend some time studying Android ideas for app development in the near future. But, you'll need to begin thinking about the things you'd like to build your Android application for. What is the need you want to tackle in your app? Does your app plan to simply be an extension of your existing website--a version that is an app of your website, or will it be a source of distinct information? What is your market? What is your competition? If you're looking at receiving a lot of downloads for your app, then you'll have to make sure you are near the very top in the Google Play

Store. If you choose an app that is surrounded by a lot of competition, you'll have to think about the way you'll compete with your competitors, the way you advertise your app and the reason users would prefer your app over others--your USP.

Chapter 2: App Ideas Generation

"Everything starts in the form of an image."

--Earl Nightengale

The most important thing to be successful in an app for Android applications is to create your thoughts and plan out the way you'll implement it. All things begin by generating an initial idea.

The initial Android application I developed might seem random and unintentional, but it was the niche market and had very little competition of quality, and there was a massive demand. The market I picked to target was Nigerian Movies, or as they're referred to, "Nollywood Movies." Nollywood is the second-largest film industry and is the most popular in terms of the number of films. While I'm not Nigerian but I was aware of this as an excellent niche to target. I had an online site which was a repository for Nigerian Movies which was getting between 4 and 6 thousand people every day, so I was aware of the market. It made sense to design an application that could connect to this market, and also make it simpler for both visitors and users to watch the movies they wanted to see. I utilized the same tools that I will discuss throughout this guide to develop this application. The initial concept became a huge hit. The app was popular; it became the top app within its class on Google Play. Google Play store and was downloaded more than 500 times each day, with the total installed more than 100,000 in the initial year. After that, I expanded into that Nigerian market, to Nigerian news and current affairs, using multiple channels to cross promote all application.

What is your specialization?

Do you have something that you know from the inside? Something that you're obsessed with? If you have asked your friends what is the thing you're truly obsessed with What would they tell you? You should take a few minutes to consider something you know which you could then discuss with other people. It isn't necessary to have all the information, or even be able to write the content. It could be as simple as or it could be a cookbook with favorite recipes your mom used to cook. It could also be that you're interested in current affairs or politics or even your preferred pastime.

SEARCHING APPS FOR YOUR APP

When you've come up with an idea of a subject it is time to study to find the right market application. I'll give you an example of how I accomplish this:

I developed a particular application in this book to explain how I achieved this. The app I've launched is available on the Drone Market. I noticed my drone that I am using which is which is a DJI Phantom, has a range of different warning lights that are difficult to understand. It is helpful when on the go to understand what the warning lights mean even if there isn't internet access.

I then went to the Google Play store - https://play.google.com/store and searched for the most obvious terms a person would use to find an app about DJI LEDs. I looked up DJI lights LEDs, DJI lights, DJI warnings, etc. I then found there was really only one other app providing this information: https://play.google.com/store/apps/details?id=oz han.org.djiledsescription. I was then looking to determine the popularity of this app was. When you click an app on Store, it informs you the number of times that the app has been downloaded - in this instance, between 10,000 to 50,000. It is evident that there was an interest in the app, and competition was not that high. It was then time to assess the competition and see what I could improve or do differently. This is a simple. The app was downloaded and then had an experiment with it. I then looked at the reviews posted by other users who downloaded the app, as well as the overall rating. The app that was competing had an average rating of 3.5 The reviews included things such as "No absolutely not No. It is not possible to set an account with a preferred card! It is not possible to look at what's on the inside of the card in which you will find additional details. It could also be helpful, but not in the way it is currently, so it's better to search online." Also "Looks helpful, but it doesn't clarify if my model DJI uav is applicable, therefore I removed it. A easy model list? I'm not going to bother."

Based on these reviews and ratings the app, it's clear that by tweaking just a few aspects, including an accurate overview of DJI Drone models, and making sure that the screen that opens isn't blank could make the app more beneficial to users.

Then, I reviewed the interface of the app. Is there a video showing how to utilize the application? Do you have multiple screen shots that show how the app works? Are the descriptions a complete explanation of the app's features and its functions? In this example the app, there were only two images, but no video, and a description which states:

"- A2

- WooKong-M

- Naza-M V2

Naza-M Lite

No Addition

No Permission Needed

"Free - and Free :)"

If you're not truly knowledgeable then you'll not know what the app is and whether it will be compatible with the drone you have or not.

Now is the time to start developing some ideas to create your application. Make sure you follow these simple steps:

* Make it simple

* What is the information you are an expert in that others would like to know about?

* Examine the performance of the competition

* You don't need to write all the content by yourself.

* Design something that will help fulfill the needs of others.

AppBrain is another excellent resource for research on other Apps on the Play store. Visit http://www.appbrain.com/stats/android-market-app-categories

The list of apps includes the number of apps available in every Play store category, along with the percent of free apps and paid apps, as well as the percentage of free vs. Paid apps. There is also details on the number of apps that fall into each category as well as an average rating for stars, percent of apps that have over 50k downloads, average cost of apps and more. With this data you can determine the areas that are more or less competitive which could impact on the success that your application will enjoy.

As an example, at present (November 2016) the category of Parenting on the PlayStore includes less than 880 applications, with the top app boasting more than 10,000,000 downloads. 71 % of the 880 apps have a low rating, with just 9 percent of those with more than 10,000 downloads.

Feeds RSS for Content

A great method of receiving regular, regularly updated information is through RSS feeds.

What is an RSS Feed?

RSS is the abbreviation in the form of Rich Site Summary or more often referred to as Simply Simple Syndication. It's essentially a Web feed that can be used to refresh content and other information on websites, such as blogs, blog posts news headlines, videos as well as audio (podcasts) as well as other types of.

RSS Feeds are typically recognize by the icon above. Many websites use RSS feeds that you can subscribe to in order to stay up-to-date with their latest content. A few examples of this are:

Google News UK RSS Feed is https://news.google.co.uk/news?cf=all&hl=en&pz=1&ned=uk&output=rss

If you click the link to Google News RSS feed, if you open Google News RSS feed in your browser, it will not have any significance, however when you integrate it into your app, it will refresh all the images and news. It is possible to find the Google News feed RSS in many ways. If you access, for example, www.google.co.uk/news and scroll to the bottom of the page, you will see a link for RSS Feed.

You can also make your own RSS feed to any particular topic on Google news. It's quite easy. Find the topic you're interested in using your Google Search bar and and then click "news." The result will provide you with news on the area. Scroll down to the bottom and you'll see the link "create alert" as follows:

When you click "create an alert" it will take you to be directed to the way you would like the alert to be delivered. On the screen, there's an option dropdown that shows options. Click that to open the options. You'll need to alter the settings as shown below:

Navigate towards the "delivered to"section All you have to do is to switch the dropdown menu in the dropdown to "rss feed." You are able to alter other options if like. Click on "Create Alert" to create your alert. It will bring you to a page with the details of your RSS feed. The icon I've highlighted that holds the RSS Feed. Select the RSS icon to access you to access your RSS feed.

For instance clicking on an RSS symbol, I am presented with an RSS link that is similar to this:

https://www.google.co.uk/alerts/feeds/1002413 0363565858146/15628064237701369157

It's the RSS feed that I will incorporate into my application later. It will feed me regular news on Android apps, as well as updates as they happen.

What else can I do to find RSS Feeds?

There are many other RSS feeds online, and a simple google search on your subject and "RSS" within the results will reveal a lot of resources for you.

To locate other sources, you need to know the basics of websites can be useful. For example, if a site has been built on "Wordpress," the feed will generally be the website address, followed by "/feed." For example, the site www.greatdaysoutwithdad.com is built using

Wordpress and has an RSS feed of its contents at www.greatdaysoutwithdad.com/feed

A simple search on any website will typically provide the RSS Feed. Most often, you will find an RSS feed at the top (shown with an RSS symbol) or at the footer area of the website. If you've got a page open in Chrome when you press Control+F this will bring up a search bar where you can type in RSS.

Certain RSS feeds only give you only a "snippet" about the content as well as an image. The reader will have to click the story in order to read the entire story on the site. In most cases this is the correct option. However, there are times where you'd like to read the entire content from an RSS feed. There's an option to do this using this site:

http://fulltextrssfeed.com/

Additional sources for RSS feeds are Youtube Channels. For instance my Youtube Channel RSS feed is: RSS feed for my Youtube Channel is:

https://www.youtube.com/feeds/videos.xml?channel_id=UCuOe-vLkfdvRok9O9jSIm0g

To locate the RSS feed for the channel you want to find it, click here. Youtube Channel (as at November 2016) You must visit the channel you wish to locate the RSS feed for. Then look at the source code of the page (in Chrome, Right click on "view page source") and search for "channel-external-id" to get the value for that element. So, in the case of my channel, that is UCuOe-vLkfdvRok9O9jSIm0g. It is simply necessary to replace it with this URL:

https://www.youtube.com/feeds/videos.xml?channel_id=UCuOe-vLkfdvRok9O9jSIm0g

There are other free websites that will aid you in getting different RSS feeds. For instance, Pinterest. One website to check out is https://dlvrit.com/

Chapter 3: Making The Magic

"To create something unique you must believe that it's special."

--Mr. Ping, Kung Fu Panda

There are those who believe that there is a magical or secret formula to create your Android application. They believe that they are not capable of doing it themselves, or must learn to become a programer to be able to do it. Others think they must be a slave to an expensive web development company to take care of it. If any of these descriptions are true for you Stop now. Like I stated in the beginning that we will team up to get your first Android application completed in under 30 minutes with no knowledge of programming. It's time to start...

Beginning using AppYet

It is likely that you already have an account on Appyet. If not, sign-up by following the directions in the beginning chapter.

We will take a look at the Appyet interface as well as tools before we start creating an app. Step through to create your very first Android application.

Dashboard

If you are the first to sign into Appyet when you first sign in, you will be taken into the primary interface that will look like:

From here, you are able to access everything you require from your account. You'll see a list of your apps that are currently in use as well as version numbers, and their the current status. You can also access many other features from your account:

"My Account" will display the email address currently that is associated with your account. This it is the place to modify it if you want to. Make sure that you have a current email address that is associated with your account. In the event that you do not, you may be unable to receive notifications--for instance, if you have an update to your Android application. It is your email that is the one that the app is sent for download.

If you're looking to edit the app you've already made, clicking"details" or clicking "details" button beside the app you'd like to edit will permit you to do this.

Create app

After you click "create app" you'll be taken by this display:

From here, you'll be required to submit three details:

1. App Name. Choose the name of your app. Your "App title" is clear It is the name you'll use to name your app. For instance, "DJI LED Descriptions."

2. Package Name. The package name should be unique. Every Android apps come with an official package name. It can be the title that can uniquely identify the app on a user's smartphone or other device. It also helps distinguish the app's application in Google Play Store. Google Play Store. You are able to choose any name you like for your package name, as long as it's entirely distinctive. However, I usually employ the following naming convention for my applications as much as I can:

com.firstword.secondword

I always begin by putting "com." When you own a website, it is logical to name your app with a similar name to it. For instance, Adobe Photoshop would name their applications in this manner:

com.adobe.reader

com.adobe.photoshop

If you want to read more about App Naming Conventions, you can find out more at https://en.wikipedia.org/wiki/Java_package#Pack age_naming_conventions

3. Template. When you are creating your first app, you'll begin with a "blank the template." But, after you've created your app, you can decide to build a new app around the apps you've created.

After you've completed these sections, you'll have then click on the "create application" button.

General Dashboard

When you click on "create application" in appyet, and verified whether you've created an unique name for your package You will be taken to the next General Screen:

Name of the package. The first thing you will see on the interface is the name of your package. For the purpose of this guide, I have called my package "com.create.android.app.course."

Name of the app. My application is known as "HOW to build an ANDROID APP in 30 minutes for FREE."

You should be able to see your package's name as well as the name of your app.

Localize. In our initial Android application, we'll bypass the link that says "localize" since we don't require it.

Version name. This helps you determine the version you're working on. It is obvious that you start with 1.0 and then work your way to the next level as you make modifications and edits.

Version Code. In this course, it is possible to leave it out as it's automatically created for you.

Application Icon. The icon is displayed on the user's mobile device, tablet or phone. It is highly likely that you'll need to alter this icon from the standard one to your custom icon in order to make your app more appealing to users.

Your icon for the app will have to be 192px by 192px You can create it using the image editor of your choice. You can get some ideas from the icons for other apps of certain apps that you already have on your personal device. These are some "flat icon" ideas for design inspiration taken from various apps

Here is an illustration of the icon for the app I've created to demo my app:

Alternately, you can hire someone else to create the icon for you. A good source for design is Fiverr https://www.fiverr.com/s2/3b2fe1ca3c --as the name suggests, you could get a decent designer for $5. We'll talk in a subsequent chapter on how to locate the best graphic designers for your apps.

To upload your own icon, you'll be required to click "Change icon" then "Choose the file" to choose the icon that you've created and saved.

If you decide you don't wish to return to the icon for apps that is provided by appyet, just click "Reset back to the default."

Notification Icon. In our case of creating your first application in just 30 minutes, we'll keep this as its default icons. You may however want to switch this icon by putting your custom notification symbol that will show up in the notifications of your users whenever your content is updated. To do this, just follow the same process that you used for the icon for your app. The dimensions of this icon need to be 48px 40px by 48px.

Header image. With us completing your app for the first time in under 30 minutes, we'll keep this image as your default image for the head. If you decide to alter this, this will be the image you will use as the app's head. It will require at least 512px by 288px. It must be an appropriate pattern that allows you to navigate content efficiently.

Content Rating. All apps on the Play Store need to be assessed. You'll need to create an appropriate rating, however you must also create your rating within your Google Play Store by using the questionnaire for app ratings. It must be a true rating. False ratings could be altered by Google and I've discovered that frequently doing it wrong could cause your app to be removed by Google and removed from in the Play Store.

Full details of the app ratings can be found from the Google Content Ratings for App and Games here:
https://support.google.com/googleplay/android-developer/answer/188189?hl=en

Once you've completed this section, you'll have to select "Save the changes." Appyet will then upload any icons or images you've modified.

Settings

The next thing to check after you've saved your modifications will be "settings." It is possible to get to that via this page:

Then, you'll be taken to the dashboard screen that is shown on the next screen:

It might appear intimidating However, the settings are rational. Let's look at each setting one by one.

String Resources. They can be used in place by default, and they aren't employed, unless in more complicated applications.

Display Language. Choose the language of your application from the drop-down list. There are a variety of translations for the app that are available. If you set this setting on auto mode, the application will automatically select the appropriate one according to your settings.

Display display the language. This option is default. We'll keep it set to. It will display a screen within the app's settings that allows your users to to select the preferred language to use. This is extremely useful to the app's functionality and will allow you to market your app to various market.

Splash Screen. This is a setting that you have to choose. It is by default turned off. If you check the box and click the button, it will display an image that users will see each when they launch your application. You'll need to create an image to display this, with the ideal size being 150px by 150px. Also, you will need to choose the background color of your splash screen. The color should be set to the # colour. You can pick one of the color pickers or create your own color using the correct code that matches your website or images. There is a useful resource at http://html-color-codes.info/ to help pick your colour. Then, you'll need to choose the time period during which that the user will be presented with the splash screen prior to when they're taken to the application. Be sure to use this feature be cautious as you wish to create a seamless experience for your users that allows them to quickly get access to your information. As you use this, you might want to test different options-- with/without/longer and shorter. To test our app

I'll use this splash page to market this book as well as the online course which comes with it.

The default theme. By default, you can choose the option of choosing a light or dark themes for your application. This is your personal preference. You can also create your personal themes later using the menu of themes.

Sync Interval. If your application will have dynamic content, such as or from a feed on your site or an RSS feed, YouTube feed or youtube feed, etc. You must determine how often your app will synchronize this information. This is outlined in this article. It can be disabled , or it could be anything from 3 minutes to every 24 hours and in any time between. It's not recommended to sync too often due to many reasons. In the end, if you sync often, you'll end up consuming a lot of the data your users have (which may not be appreciated by them) If you're updating a feed often, you'll be making use of a large portion of the websites that host the feed's information. In certain cases, they may end your access to the feed. In our demo application I'll set this to run at one hour intervals.

The app will sync at startup. It's a good idea to connect the app at startup, which is why this checkbox must be checked.

Article, Image, and Download WiFi Only. By default, these options are not marked, and the user can modify these settings at the time the app is developed. I'd recommend not altering these settings. The only reason to consider changing them is if you tried to cut down on your data usage users use with the mobile data plan.

Display notifications. It displays a message to your users whenever there are updates to the app's content. Like we said you can decide the way that notifications are displayed in the settings.

New article open. The reason for this feature is to let you choose what the user sees when there's new content available in your application. This defaults to "all unreads" and is an excellent option for our demo application. It is possible, however, to prefer to change it into "last open, " e.g., what the user's last read or "last for 24 hours."

Keep those starred posts unread. One feature of your first application will allow users to be able to "star" or in essence highlight content for later reading they want to read later. It's possible to enable it so whatever they highlight is "unread." The app will leave this feature unchecked.

Auto Cleanup Read. It is a great alternative for an application which is producing a large amount of content. For instance, if you were running a news application which provided content via an RSS feed (e.g., RSS Feed). When a user has finished reading an article in the feed, you could configure the app to automatically clean and delete the article from the device of the user to save space your app consumes. The app defaults this to never, however you can choose to set it from daily to every couple of days or every couple of weeks. When you've got your app running in accordance with the content, you may be interested in reviewing the feedback received from users who have used your app.

Auto Cleanup unread. This operates exactly in the same way as auto cleanup read and it performs the same functions with the exception of articles that the user has not read.

Feedback Email. It will be an email through which users can reach you with any questions, suggestions or problems. It is beneficial to have an email address created to handle this type of request for your applications. In the event that you do not, you could get unwanted emails on your private account.

Help Link. In order to make our first app that launches in 30 minutes, we'll leave the link blank. However, if you intend to provide your customers with a guide to help/faq to the app, include the link here and users will be granted access to it by using the help menu within your application. The link should point to an area on your website. In our demo application I'm going to link to the website that is included with this book.

Google Analytics. It allows you to monitor usage data for your application and will assist you with your analytics such as being able to determine where your customers are located, their demographics, sources and the most visited pages within your application, etc. When you are adding Google Analytics code you must add it in the format the form UA-12345678-1, for instance. You can get a code for this direct from the Google Analytics website at www.google.com/analytics. In our demonstration we've left the field blank. However, when you create new apps, you'll need to use this feature to gain more insight into your apps and enhance your app.

"Save Changes" to save the settings "Save Changes" to save the settings.

The settings are in place for us to begin creating your app. So you can go out and have a drink, and we'll begin creating your content for your app for the first time!

MODULE ADD

The app you create will be made out of "modules." Every module acts as the menu within your app that pulls information. This could be hard-coded data, for instance, something similar to an image, a Word document or image. You could also incorporate feeds (RSS feeds, like the ones mentioned earlier) into your application. In the first version of our Android app, we'll be importing feeds of data to begin with.

To begin to begin, you must hit"module" in the "module" submenu. This will open the dashboard:

If you were to create this app right now you'd have an app that would appear as follows:

There are some essential features that have been which are included by default in your application. They all are linked to the menu of modules. They are automatically included, but you can toggle them off or on or delete them all if you want. This provides you with a number of very effective possibilities for app development and creative thinking.

We'll begin at the very bottom of the list of the modules already available on your application, and we will go over what they do and what capabilities they offer.

Explore

The explore module permits users to upload their own content using feeds into your app. This is an extremely useful feature that allows users to personalize the application. Additionally, it allows them to take away any settings you've let them change.

If you click "details" in Explore, if you click on "details" next to Explore module you are able to modify the module. The same is true for any module, both the default ones as well as any new ones that you'll be making.

The settings can be changed to display this screen:

A couple of simple settings that are easily changed. When you click "icon picker" you are able to select from a pre-defined set of icons that represent the module in your application. If you choose "icon upload" it is possible to along with other icons and images within your app, upload your own icon following the same procedure like before. When you choose to upload your own image the size must be 72px x 72px.

"Order," as the name suggests is the order in which this module will appear within your application. One simple trick can be to boost the number of your modules by 10s. If in the future you'd like to swiftly introduce a new module between two modules it is possible to make this happen without having to renumber all your other modules.

"Enabled" (by the default, ticked) indicates it will automatically be activated within your app as it's created. If you do not tick this box button, the menu is not displayed in your app. However, you can activate it again in future builds if wish to reinstate it.

"Order" as well as "Enabled" are the standard settings that can be altered in any of your modules with the same process.

Settings

These let your users modify any default settings of the app. The device of the user will display the display will look like this:

It is advisable to enable the settings module to be enabled to allow users to control their own experience within the app.

"Synchronization" is a function that "synchronisation" function lets the user modify the default settings you previously set around the sync interval or background sync, start-up sync, etc.

"Notifications" permit the user to disable or enable the settings you had enabled previously in the area of notifications. It also allows notifications to send out messages using the use of sound, vibration, or light.

"about" option gives you your contact information "about" option provides your personal information as an app's developer.

Themes

This module lets the final user to select the theme they would like to select; it will display the user the "switch theme" option.

Sync

The Sync module lets a user to synchronize the most current feeds and information within the app. This should also be set to "activated."

Downloads

This feature allows users the ability to store any information in your app to read offline at a later time. It's a very useful option for your application.

Other modules consist of an assortment of placeholders and dividers to additional modules when these are added. Of course, you can modify and edits, or deletes from them as needed for future app development.

The focus will now be specifically on what is called the "New Module" section that is located at the bottom of this page.

In our first app we'll include a few various modules that will give users a taste of how you can build your application. The first module that we'll include is a generic "Feed/RSS."

Select "Feed (RSS/Atom)," that will take you to the next screen:

"Menu title" is the name of the Module that will appear on your app's menu. "Menu name" will be the title of your menu "Menu Order" is the place where this item will be displayed in the list of items on your app.

In my app demo I will include an RSS Feed that contains information concerning Android software via Google news. Make sure to add the feed's name in the menu's name (we discussed RSS feeds in the previous book) Select and make an place an order for this item on our menu. Then, select "save." Save will bring up this menu for you to personalize the information regarding the new RSS feed:

Although it might appear that there are many menu options available, in reality we'll walk you through every option step-by-step. It's an easy process to follow.

First, you must add the RSS Feed URL. In this case, I'll include:

https://www.google.co.uk/alerts/feeds/1002413 0363565858146/3608214532947161319

Article Limit Number

This limit the number of stories that are added to the feed prior to when the app begins to automatically delete old unread and read stories. You can alter the default settings within the dropdown menu from keeping the unread stories, up to 10, all the way to 2000. Be aware of these settings regarding the user-friendliness of your app. Having a lot of stories that go not read could make it hard for users to locate the content they want to read and reduce their use of your app.

DisQus Comments

DisQus is a different comments system where users can leave comments on feeds and other things within your application. As a default for our demo app, we leave this option unchecked. However, should you wish to enable it, you will need to ensure that you have a DisQus account which you can create at http://www.disqus.com

View image using Touch

If there are images within your feed and a user clicks on an image it will allow them to see the larger image within your application.

Minimum image width/minimum image height

To make it easier for us to test application, we'll set this to 100 by 100. As you look at how you can customize your apps in the future you might want to alter this in accordance with the layout you want to use.

Show view on the website

In default, this option is checked, but this is an individual choice. In a nutshell, this will display your feed's source at the conclusion of the article inside the app.

Open in default browser

This is by default checked. I prefer to remove this because it forces users away from the app to their normal web browser. When it's ticked, it means that when users click that link in order to open the article in your newsfeed, it will take users to their default web browser to access the news feed.

Show Translate

It gives the user the option of translating your feed, which is a valuable feature for those who download your app. This will help you expand the market for your app.

Copy link to show

This feature will also improve the usability of your app. It also allows users to share contents of your app.

Show the world that you are sharing

One way to increase the number of downloads for your app is by encouraging the use of the app and its content. This is by default checked, and I'd advise you to always make this option available.

Show Publisher

Show publisher performs exactly as it says on the label: it shows the name of the person who created the RSS feed that you have in your application. This is by default checked.

Let delete

It allows users to cleanse the newsfeed in their app by simply deleting articles from their feed. Another option that is useful, which allows complete user-specific customization of the application.

The following options, Encoding, Additional Html Header, Add Jquery and Feed GUI do not require any modification within the basic setup of your app.

By clicking "update" is going to update the module and include the module in your application.

For a quick overview Once you have added the first RSS Feed following the steps we've gone over It will then make these adjustments to the front of your application:

When you open the app, it will appear as follows:

This will now show the news feed from your feed of news that you've added to your module.

The three dots located at the top of that page will present your user with the following choices:

This allows the user to remove, hide, or modify the layout and sync of the feed to suit their personal preferences.

By clicking on the article, you will reveal more information from the feed's information:

This displays the article view with the options activated (by hitting the triangle to the top right of the screen for the article).

The options we previously set are available here: translate, permit users to delete articles or copy the link, and share. You can also change the size of the font for better accessibility.

The first one you created is in operation and is active. Let's look at the other kinds of modules.

Web module

On the lower right of the module's main screen (if you're not there, click "module" in the upper menu) then click "web."

Each module has the same format for setting up. In the beginning, you'll be directed to the screen where you can give the module a name. Menu name: name your module. In our application I'm going to make this web-based module it is the Appyet Image cheat sheets. The module, in my case will be referred to as "Image cheat sheets." Name it something that is relevant to your app. The order of the menu, similar to different modules, will be the way this module will appear in the menu. Click save.

Your next display you be able to see will look something like this:

There are two options: you can make an own "web page" that will display users when they click the link:

In order to do this, in essence creating your page in the same way as you create a Word document. You can add text, change the image's size and styles, fonts, tables as well as links to other pages , upload images and many more.

For my webpage I will create a table using this icon:

A pop-up window will open that allows you to create your table:

Table properties are fairly straightforward. The only thing you need to know is handful of options to examine when you begin. It is possible to look over another setting while you build your the next apps. The number in rows is how many rows that your table will contain.

Columns refers to how many columns that your table will contain.

Border refers to the width of the table's cells.

Align is a dropdown that lets you select which table should be aligned to the page.

Width is the measurement of how wide the table will span over the entire page. Keep in mind the size of your screen device's viewers. Height is a choice until you decide to enforce the user to have a certain height.

After you have set your table's settings Click OK, and it will be added to your website's content page. Then, you can add your own content to the table. Here's an illustration that shows how the demonstration appears:

You can certainly include any additional content, alter colors, etc. To upload an image, you'll need to click:

When you click that, it will open you these choices:

Image Info Tab

URL The URL is the hyperlink to the image that you would like to add. The image must already be on the internet. If it is not already online, you could upload it to an image hosting site, for example, http://www.imgur.com. The URL should look like this:

http://i.imgur.com/bElgS3O.png

Clicking on the small refresh icon (to to the right of the padlock icon) it will give you an image preview.

The dimensions that the image originally had can be displayed. You can however alter the dimensions of the image. Also, to improve usability for the user it is essential to ensure that the settings look great on mobile devices.

Alternative text: This can be a a good practice and you need to include some information about the image in the event it fails to load, or for people who are unable to load images.

Align: Once again, this allows you to decide which way the image should be aligned with the page.

The link tab at the top of the page: If you wish the image to hyperlink to a different page upon clicking then you can include the URL to that page in URL. Target lets you choose whether the image is displayed in a new app window, the same window, etc.

When you click"OK" you'll see something that looks like this:

Start creating your own content.

Below the box for adding your content, there is a checkbox "Show an ad." This checkbox is not checked by default. We'll be discussing the possibility of monetizing your app through the bonus sections of this book. In the meantime, we'll not check this box. Clicking "save modifications" is a way to save changes in your program.

By clicking on "Back to Modules" will bring you to the modules screen , and the next step.

Another option for web content creation is to create a link to a website. When you click the new web module "web" after you've given your the module a name as well as an order from the menu, you'll be taken to the page that we've been looking at. But, on the top that there is an option called "type," and there is a dropdown. If you click the dropdown and select "web hyperlink," you can simply connect to an existing page, for instance on your existing website. There are a variety of options this is available and also to earn money.

Your app will look as follows to the final user:

This is the way the menu appears. Look at below the "Image Cheat Sheet" which is a link to the table we designed. I also changed the menu for the image we made in the web content . It will be referred to as "App Meme images." The menu's first item, the image cheat sheets, display another screen.

This table was made by following the steps above to insert a 5x5 table within web content.

This is the web content page for images that we made by including the image in the web content module.

We are currently building our first prototype app that includes some dynamic content taken from our RSS feeds, static images, as well as static content.

Wordpress Feed Module

It is incredibly simple to incorporate the Wordpress feed to your application. If the app you are building is built using Wordpress it is an extremely simple way to integrate all your most recent posts into your app.

Similar to before, at lower right of the main screen for modules (if you're not there, just click "module" in to the upper menu) then click to open "WordPress feed."

The menu will appear:

Simply fill in the form, like before "Menu Name," which is what you'll name the item, and then click the hyperlink on your WordPress website.

After this, click "next" after which the usual menu will pop up informing you to change your feed with the amount of articles, images dimensions, share options, etc. Similar to other modules you've installed. If you're stuck, you can refer back to the guidelines for setting up new modules.

Now you have the foundation of your first amazing Android application. If you take a look at our application the menu appears pretty basic. The icons in our menus are dull and basic. We're now going to go into the other settings within the menu and module options.

Navigate to your Modules screen by clicking "modules" on the bar of options for your application.

We're now planning to tweak our modules. This process is similar for each module that is available.

Then, to the right, select "Details." We're going to alter the settings of the very first module we designed, "Android App News." When you click "details" brings to a menu which will look something like this:

The menu icon selection lets you customize your icons for menu items. You can choose "icon selector" by clicking the checkbox which will provide you with a drop-down listing of the default icons you can choose from a selection of more than 1300.

You can also create or upload your personal icon, by leaving "Icon upload" selected and pressing

"Change icon." Follow the same process for uploading another images to upload your own custom icon. Dimensions must be set to 72px x 72px.

Standard layout: There's several drop-down options available here that allow you to alter the default layout of your feed's content.

We will also mark the "explore" box , which will let users remove any feeds from the apps through settings, if they wish to.

We've looked at some possibilities to set up modules. To further develop your app it is necessary to include several different modules in line with the ones we've discussed so far. Other modules, like, Pinterest, Wordpress, and so on. They all use the same structure.

After you've included all the modules you'd like in your application You must ensure that they're in the correct order. To check this you need to go back to the Modules main menu and click on "Modules" in the top menu. When you open your application, you'll be able to see the order that of the items on your menu are placed in. If you'd like to alter this order, the little arrows in"Sort Order "Sort order" on every menu (menu) item allows users to alter the order. If you'd like to swiftly turn off any menu item then you can deactivate it off from "Enabled" which means it will not be included when you create your application.

Develop your application

Once you've completed adding every module and modification to your app, you're now ready to create your application.

You can access the Build menu by clicking "Build":

There's one thing to know about here. If you're building your application in the very first instance, just go ahead and click "Submit to Build"--your application will be developed and then sent to you in just a few minutes.

If you're upgrading an app that you have already installed you can use this option for users to notify users of what's changed. Select "edit" under "What's changing" to provide the user with an update on the changes made when they update and then open the application.

Once you've clicked "submit to build" you will be able to see the following:

It will inform you the progress of your app in the process of being developed, with a status of pending. It will also tell the time the process will last. When the work is complete, your initial app will be delivered at your address.

You've got it, your first Android app developed in under 30 minutes! Congratulations!

Chapter 4: Installation Testing

"Manufacturing involves more than making parts. The process involves coming up for ideas as well as testing concepts and advancing the engineering process, and finally, the assembly."

James Dyson

We did it! We developed our first Android app and it's sitting within your email inbox... What next?

First, if the app did not arrive in your email, make sure you check all your folders, including the junk/spam folder, in case the message was sent by mistake.

The email will include details of your app together with the application as an unzip file. The typical email will read like this:

The most efficient method to test your application is to check your email using your Android Device. If you are using a smartphone or tablet, click on the document to install it.

The file is one of the formats, namely a Zip therefore you might get a warning to be cautious when downloading files that you need to confirm for.

After downloading your zip files, you'll be required to launch it using double-clicking on it. Certain Android devices will unzip the file for users to open it. However, in other devices, you'll require an app to perform the task for you. I use ES File Explorer, available for free from the play store here: https://play.google.com/store/apps/details?id=com.estrongs.android.pop&hl=en_GB

Once the zip file is unzipped (if required) Click upon to install the Android Package (your app) to install it.

You will receive an error message that reads like "Install Blocked for security. your phone has been set to prevent installation of apps that are downloaded from untrusted source." This can only occur when trying to test the application by installing it directly on your phone. It won't happen when you download the app through Play Store. Play store. You'll need to go into the settings of your device, normally under security. Here's how to do it:

Set the setting to "Unknown Sources." Allow installation of apps that come from other sources than the Play Store.

If you permit this option, you should get the option to "Allow for this application only." If you do not, it is important to remember to modify the setting once you have installed the application.

It will then guide you through installing the app just similar to any other app that it downloads from Play store.

Once you've completed this, a symbol will be displayed on your device that will start the app. Open the app and experience your initial Android app!

It is essential to test all your menus, alter the settings, and then test your application to ensure that it works exactly as you expect it to. Make sure there aren't any broken links to pages or images. Feeds will refresh gradually over the next few minutes following the initial load. As they refresh regularly then you should see the notification icon pop up if you've left the settings on. If you find that something doesn't work as you would expect, or you'd like to alter or modify something, you can go back to appyet and make the changes to your app. Rebuild, download, and then reinstall the app to make sure everything is what you'd like it to be.

Chapter 5: Get It On Play

"If you create it, he will arrive."

"Field of Dreams

We've completed our first Android application in less than 30 minutes. We've developed it, it's going to be easy for people to be able to use it and use it, right? Wrong! It is essential to make your app accessible for take advantage of and download. The subsequent bonus chapters, like this one, discuss making your application accessible to download from Google Play and how to earn money through your app.

Starting using Google Play

With more than 2.5 million apps with over 2.5 million apps, the Google Play Store is where the majority of users download their apps. There are other sites where users can download apps, however the preferred choice for downloading apps is in the Play Store.

It's very simple to set up the Playstore Account to add your application in the Playstore marketplace. Follow the link to https://play.google.com/apps/publish/signup/

You'll need to set up an Google Play Publisher Account. It will cost you an initial fee of $25. There is no requirement to pay annual registration fees or other fees. This is in contrast to other apps. Apple AppStore.

If you plan to sell your app, or other in-app products then you'll also have to create a Google Pay Merchant Account. Google takes 30 percent of sales , with you keeping about 70 percent.

Follow the steps on the screen, and make the payment to have your account up and running. When you first sign into Google's Developer Console you'll be able to see the following:

As you can see in the example I have provided, all applications you've installed previously will be displayed here, with the information about current installations along with the average rating as well as other pertinent information. Downloads to Active Devices (devices that have been online for the last 30 days with this application installed)/Total Users Installed (total amount of users who have installed this application on any on their device).

It is necessary to click "+ Add New Application" on the right side to start setting up your application. It will look something like this:

Input the title of your app It must not exceed 30 characters. Then click "Prepare the Store Listing."

It is possible to go straight to uploading your app but we'll prepare your store's listings first.

Now, we will guide you through the process of setting up the Play Store listing in sections:

You'll notice some subheadings left on the left: APK, Manage Releases, etc. If the ticks that are circled are not in the right place, you won't be able publish your app on the store. So, it is necessary to look through each section step-by-step. Beginning with The Store Listing.

In the upper right hand corner of the name of your application you'll see the option to change the language for the description of your app. If you click on it, it will allow you to choose a different option to change the language and you can manage several languages using an option called "Manage Translation" drop down menu.

The app's title can be pre-populated. If you wish to alter the title or title of the app, here's how you can do it.

The title of your app appears on your Play Store listing when someone seeks your app. It is important to keep it brief and concise, no more than 80 characters and one that is sure to grab the attention of users. You can also include terms that users might be using to locate your site, you should not use them to promote your app. There is some guidance offered in this section available directly from Google here: https://play.google.com/about/storefront-promotional.html#metadata

The Full Description is where you write the complete details of your app, up at 4000 words. This is an excellent location to promote your app to prospective users , and also to showcase the benefits and features the app offers. It's not the best location to provide reviews of your app, as they are covered in the user rating your app. It is recommended to use your complete description to describe what you love about your app, and perhaps fascinating details on the reasons you came up with the app. Keep your app's description short and simple. The shorter descriptions improve the user experience, particularly for devices with smaller screens.

Scrolling down will bring us to the option of adding graphic assets to your store's page:

It is necessary to create an array of images that will be displayed on your Play Store to promote your app. When you launch your first app you may need to design these by yourself. Alternatively, you could go to https://www.fiverr.com/s2/3b2fe1ca3c and find a graphic designer who could do this for you.

The complete details of how the images are utilized can be located here:

https://support.google.com/googleplay/android-developer/answer/1078870

You should submit at minimum two screen shots of your application in your listing. The images must be stored as JPG as well as PNG format. The easiest method of doing this is to launch the application from the Android smartphone and saving a snapshot. Then, you can upload the photo to the Play store's listing. To make your photos distinguish themselves from rest it is possible to use a free tool that is available at https://placeit.net. Placeit lets you upload a photo that appears like it's in place on the device, such as:

The screenshots you upload will be displayed on the app's page of details within Google Play's website and app. Google Play website and Android application.

The next pictures you'll need to submit are hi-re icon and the Graphics for Feature Graphic as well as the Promo Graphic as well as the TV Banner. It is also possible to add the URL of a Youtube video of your application in case you have one.

The Hi-res icon appears at various locations in the Play Store. It doesn't replace the icon of your app that is that is installed on the device of the user The Hi-res icon is an improved representation of your logo that is 512 by 512 pixels, stored as PNG.

It is the Feature Graphic is a really important picture to have on your listing. It appears in the middle of the listing's page on the store. If you've linked to a video in your app, the image will also feature an overlay of a Play button. The image can be uploaded in or JPG or png, and it must be at least 1024 x 500 pixels. When creating this image, make sure not to include any crucial information within the bottom part of your image because it could be lost.

It is important to note that the Promo Graphic is only shown on versions of Android older than 4.0 and does not require for upload.

Scrolling down takes our attention to the "contacts and privacy policies" on the Play Store listing:

This section is pretty straightforward. The first step is to decide whether your app is an "application" or an "game." In this example, I've selected application. The next step is to choose the appropriate category for your app from the dropdown. Then, you need to select an appropriate content rating from the drop-down menu that includes everyone from High Maturity. There is a full breakdown of ratings to help you correctly list your app here: https://support.google.com/googleplay/android-developer/answer/188189

It is definitely worth the effort to go through the rating guidelines, particularly the last paragraph, "Previous rating system," in relation to these ratings in particular.

Once you have completed the assessment and have completed the rating, you will need to enter your contact information. If, however, you don't have a website or privacy policy then you don't have to fill in these. Additionally, if your app handles sensitive or personal user data, there may be other requirements for having an privacy policy you must keep in your mind.

Scroll up to the top and click "Save Draft."

Once you've saved draft, you'll see that the tick in front of "Store Listing" has not been visible. It is now greyed out. If it's grayed out, scroll down to make sure whether you missed any section.

If you look at the menu left there is a category that is known as APK. Android Application Package (APK) refers to the file format utilized for an application running on the Android operating system to distribute as well as installation of mobile applications. This is the app you was previously sent via email. Before you upload it, you'll have first "unzip" this file from your personal computer. After that, you'll be required in order to download the file. This will be named the same as the one you gave it in the process of setting up your application .apk.

After it has been completed processing and uploaded After that, you'll be able to be able to see the tick next APK change to green.

On the leftside, click "Content Evaluation." The section you are looking for is easy to understand; it's a survey to make sure your app is properly evaluated. Once you've completed it, hit save, next click "Calculate the rating" to obtain the app a rating in the Google Play Store. Scroll down after that , and then select "apply the rating."

The next part we'll explore is to the left side and is called "Pricing and Distribution." The section will be like this:

There's a lot in this, but it's not as overwhelming as it seems.

In the beginning, you need to choose if you would like an app either free or paid. If you choose free, your app will remain free and you are not able to charge for it later. If you choose to pay the app will like the previous paragraph, require an account for merchants.

Choose the countries you would like your application to be available to. If there's no restriction then click "Select every country."

The first app currently is free of advertisements. But, we'll be looking to add advertisements in our next section of bonuses. So , if you're planning to include ads, make sure you tick "yes that it contains ads."

Now, you can scroll towards the category "Google Play for Education." If the app you're developing falls into the criteria, you'll be able to mark this box. If you've created your own Android or Chrome application that could be ideal for schools, or even have an idea of one, you must be aware of Google Play for Education. Google Play for Education is an online platform for teachers who can easily find, buy, and distribute apps to their students in only two clicks.

This is followed by"consent" "consent" part. Marketing opt out will stop your app from being advertised anywhere other than the Play Store.

It is important to ensure that your app is in compliance with the guidelines for content. If you're satisfied then you can be in agreement with the guidelines in the "Content Guidelines box."

In addition, you must acknowledge that the software you use for your application is bound by United States export laws, regardless of your place of residence or country of residence.

Once more, scroll until you reach the top and select "Save Draft." A green checkmark shouldn't appear on the right side of Pricing and Distribution.

This means you see a green highlighted tick in the APK section, next to Content Rating, Store Listing and Pricing and Distribution. Now is the time to launch your application. The button at the top which was greyed out previously should be available now to click "Publish application" (next step is to save draft). This is it! Within a couple of hours and a few minutes, your first Android app will be made available to everyone to download from the Play Store.

Chapter 6: How To 'Apply Money' Your App

" To be rich, you need to earn money while asleep."

--David Bailey

After you have a good foundation for creating your app, you'll likely want to consider ways to make money from your app.

Making money from your app is much simpler than you think. This is a easy guide to earning money from your app.

First, log back into Appyet.com and then, in the main menu "my applications" after you sign in, click "details" on the right side of the app you have installed.

In the upper menu Click on "monetize." The click will open the menu with a number of choices to choose from:

Click on the dropdown beside "Ad type:" and you will be presented with a variety of ways to make money from your application. We will examine Google Admob. Please do, though, visit my website at www.cheshirecreativepublishing.com where I will be adding how-to guides for other monetization options.

Choose Google Admob.

You'll require an Admob account for free in order to include ads in your application. The best part about this is that you don't have to search for the ads you want to place ads on your app. Services like Admob can do this for you. Go to https://www.google.com/admob/ to setup an AdMob account if you don't have one already.

Once you've got the account set up, go to the monetize area in Admob:

Hit the red icon "+ Monetize a new app."

Then, you'll be presented with an the option of adding your application:

Choose "add your application by hand" from the menu at the top. In the box that is given, enter the name of your application. After that, you must choose Android from the drop-down listing "platform."

The button to add apps is now accessible. Click it to continue.

The first step is to select first, choose banner. Then, you can choose which ads will be either images, text or both by selecting the boxes. You can also alter how often the ads are refreshed (or modified). It is now time to put in the Ad unit's name, or a title that helps you remember which ad it is. Then click save.

You will now have an add unit name that will look like this: ca-app-pub-12345678910/12345678910

Copy the ID of the ad unit. Be sure to copy the app ID.

Then go back to Appyet where we started and type in the ID of the ad unit in the "Admob Banner Ad Unit ID:" section under monetize/admob in Appyet.

If you'd like to include Interstitial advertisements (Interstitial ads display full screen advertisements that are able to cover the entire interface of the application they're hosted by. They're usually shown at natural transition points in the flow of the application, for example between tasks or in the interval between levels in games) If you want to do this, go again to Admob and select "Create an additional advertisement component" at the end of the page you were on.

The next time, from the menu, choose "interstitial" and do the same like you did before. When you hit "save," again you will be given a brand fresh Ad unit ID that you will need in order to paste it into your section of appyet called of Admob's interstitial Ad unit ID. In Appyet you have to decide where advertisements will be displayedbe cautious not to add excessive ads since it could distract your users and impact the overall user experience in your application.

Select "Save Changes." Your app is now complete and ready to run advertisements. It is now time to build your application. Select "build," then click on "Submit to Build." Like previously, your program will now be rebuilt, and then emailed to you. It is also necessary to upload another version into the Play Store If you've already uploaded your application. This is done by returning to the The Google Play Developer Console, and clicking "APK," then "upload the new APK into production."

Chapter 7: The Word Is: Spread

"If you create your own website... it might require Google AdWords." --Jennifer Mesenbrink

About 700,000 apps have been released to the Play store in the last year. There was an average of about 45,000 new apps added on the Play Store every month for the last six months, you will face plenty of competition to make your app visible.

We'll explore a few basic strategies to help you market your app. For more in depth ideas, tips, and tricks, visit my website at www.cheshirecreativepublishing.com or the Facebook group at https://www.facebook.com/groups/createyouran droidapp/

You'll want to make the most of the possibility that your app is new to the Play Store. One of the things you must achieve is to gain as many downloads as you can in those first couple of days after the launch.

Be Reviewed

An easy and quick method to get your app first noticed is to get your app evaluated. Some sites that do this include http://mobilestartupz.com/, http://www.appstoreapps.com/

Join a social network!

Sharing is caring, they say... When you have your app, sharing is important. Find information about your app via social media websites which include Twitter, Facebook, Google Plus, Linked in, and so on. There are other bookmarking websites. If you have not come across these before, take a look at www.stumbleupon.com and https://www.reddit.com/

Get Free

You can ask blogs, websites, and Facebook pages that are related to applications for technology and mobile. For example, http://mobilestartupz.com/ is an app community where users vote and rank apps on a monthly basis.

Create a Facebook Page or Website

If you do not have a site You can easily purchase an domain name and build an initial landing page for it. Alternately, you can create a Facebook page to promote your app for free. You can even add the link on the page in your app to have users and other users talking regarding your application.

Find some ads

There are a lot of locations where you can spend money to promote your brand's new app. Some of the ones I've tested that have produced excellent outcomes include Facebook Ads. You can use them to drive the app's installs and pay for the results. You can also promote on Google with Google Adwords or Admob.

Join the Search

After you have the app's URL on the Play Store, it is recommended to upload it to the standard search engines, such as Google.com, Bing.com, and Yahoo.com.

Chapter 8: The Select Statement

If we need to search our database we make use of the query SELECT. This allows us to access specific information based on the specific criteria you specify. The SELECT statement contains five clauses. The only one that's necessary can be from clause. Each clause comes with a variety of options, parameters and choices and is listed below. I'll provide more details about the clauses in the following chapter.

The structure for a statement using SELECT can be described around like this:

* Select DISTINCT] column1[. FROM table1[,table2][WHERE "conditions"is a grouping of "column-list" [HAVING "conditions [ORDER by "column-list" ASC

A good instance of the WHERE and FROM clauses are:

* SELECT name, age, salary

* FROM employee

* WHERE AGE > 50 years old;

This query is asking you to choose the values that are in the columns requested by the table. For this example Name, Age, and Salary for all employees who are over 50 years old.

Do not forget to end your statement by putting an apostrophe as this is an indication that your sentence is complete and prepared for interpretation.

Comparison Operators

Equal

> Greater Than

< Less Than

>= greater than or Equal to

*= Less Than or Equal to

• Or not equal to

LIKE String Comparison Test

Note Concerning LIKE

* SELECT name, title, dept. FROM the employee WHICH title is "Pro%"

This command will display all rows and values of the columns named Name Title, Name as well as Dept.-where the title begins with PRO.

All and DisTINCT are additional keywords that can be employed to select the entire as well as distinct (unique) documents. If you wish to find unique records from particular columns, you must make use of the DISTINCT keyword. This will remove duplicate records within the specified columns:

* SELECT DISTINCT AGE

* FROM employee_info;

This is a request to see all records that are unique in the column titled "age" of the employee data table.

The ALL keyword will return all records, regardless of regardless of whether they're duplicates, or not. If not other options are specified, it will be an default configuration.

Aggregate Functions

MIN Returns the lowest value of any column

MAX Returns the highest value for any column in the given column.

SUM Returns the sum of numerical values for any given column

AVG will return the average values for any column

COUNT Returns the total value in a column.

COUNT (*) Returns how many rows are in table

Aggregate functions are the ones we employ to calculate against the numeric data returned from the SELECT query. They select a particular column of data and then summarize it. We will briefly discuss these functions here since you'll need to understand them during the next chapter, and in particular that of the GROUP BY clause. The functions are able to be utilized outside within this GROUP BY clause too:

* SELECT AVG(salary)

* FROM employee;

This command will give one result , and that will be the mean value of all the values that are in the column of salary in the table for employees.

Another Example:

* SELECT AVG(salary)

* FROM employee;

* WHERE the title is 'Programmer'

This will give an average wage figure for all employees who hold the title equivalent to the title Programmer.

Another Example:

* SELECT * SELECT(*)

* FROM employees;

This function is different than the other functions due to the fact that there isn't a column in the table provided to this function. Instead, it returns the amount of rows within the table of employees.

Clauses

GROUP BY clause

This clause will gather data all rows which contain data in the columns that are specified. It also permits the aggregate functions that we spoke of earlier executed on columns, too. The most effective method to explain this is to illustrate it with an example

* column 1,

* SUM(column2)

* FROM "list-of-tables"

* GROUP by "column-list";

GROUP BY clause syntax:

Let's suppose that you wish to get information on the highest salary that is paid to each department. The statement you would write will look something like this:

* SELECT max(salary), dept.

* FROM employee

* GROUP BY dept;

The statement will reveal the highest-paid salary in each department's unique name. In short who is the individual within each department that earns the most will be shown together with their pay as well as the department they work in.

HAVING clause

The HAVING clause is one that allows you to specify specific conditions for rows within a particular group, which means that you can select specific rows can be chosen according to the particular conditions you enter. The HAVING clause must always be used in conjunction with that of the GROUP BY clause when you're using it.

HAVING clause syntax:

* Column 1, SELECT,

* SUM(column2)

* FROM "list-of-tables"

* GROUP By "column-list"

* AFFECTING "condition";

The HAVING clause should be illustrated in an example, therefore let's say your table containing all the employees' names, their department they work for along with their pay and age. If you wish to determine the average wage for each employee within every department. You could enter:

* SELECT dept., avg(salary)

* FROM employee

* GROUP BY dept;

However, let's assume that you will only determine the average and show it when their earnings are greater than $20,000. The statement you would make will look like this:

* SELECT dept, avg(salary)

* FROM employee

* GROUP BY dept

* HAVING avg(salary) > 20000;

ORDER BY clause

This clause is an optional feature and allows you to display the results of your query in an order that's ordered either ascending or decresing based on the columns you select to arrange the data.

ORDER BY clause syntax:

* Select column 1, SUM(column2) FROM "list-of-tables" ORDER by "column-list" [ASC

* [] = optional

This statement will display the employee ID department, name, age and salary in the table you select-in this instance the employee_info table where the department equals SALES. Results will be presented in ascending order, then sorted by salary.

* ASC = Ascending Order - default

*

* DESC = Descending Order

* For an example:

* SELECT employee_id, dept, name, age, salary FROM employee_info WHERE dept = 'Sales' ORDER BY salary;

If you are planning to order information from several columns, each column's name should be separated by the use of a comma

* SELECT employee_id, dept, name, age, salary

* FROM employee_info

* WHERE dept = 'Sales'

* ORDER BY salary, age DESC;

Where clause

The "where" clause can be used to limit the results that you receive within databases. It's a conditional clause. It is used to specify specific criteria for selection to choose the type of records within the table.

Syntax:

Its syntax and syntax command select along together with the clause where is described below.This will be utilized to retrieve data from tables.

SELECT field1, field2,...fieldN table_name1, table_name2..

[WHERE condition1 [AND [OR]] condition2.....

* This isn't only not limited to a single table. The "where" clause is able to be applied to multiple tables. The tables may be separated with an space. By using this, you can add the conditions by using a where clause. It is important to be aware this clause isn't an independent clause and will always be an optional component of the selection.

* Any condition is possible to specify by using the"where clause.

* By using one of the AND OR or OR operators Multiple possibilities can be made.

* This way clause isn't restricted by the clause select. It is also possible to use by using DELETE and UPDATE SQL commands.

This clause similar to an if clause that is utilized within programming languages. To compare the values given with the values of the fields in the mySQL tables, we make use of the clause where. The where clause will return one complete row in the event that the value provided from outside is equal to the field value that is available.

The complete list of operators that are able to be used as well as the "where" clause is provided below.

If field A is 10, while field B has 20. Then:

Operator Description Example

= Determines if the value of two operands match or not. If they are, then the condition is true. (A + B) is not the case.

It checks whether the operands' values are the same or not. If the values aren't equal, then the condition is true. (A = B) is true.

It checks whether the value of left operand exceeds value of right operand. If yes, then the condition is true. (A + B) is not true.

Checks to see whether the value of left operand is lower than its value the right operand. If yes, then the condition is true. (A = B) is true.

>= Checks to see if the value of left operand higher that or equivalent to its value the right

operand. If it is, then the the condition is true. (A > B) is not the case.

It checks to see if the value of left operand is less and equal to that of the right operand. If yes, then this condition will be true. (A is greater than B) is true.

The "where" clause can be utilized to retrieve certain rows from tables. Utilizing the primary key is an extensively utilized method of searching records more quickly. The query won't result in any rows in the event that the criteria specified don't coincide in the table.

Combining Boolean Operators & Conditions

If you are trying to join two or more of the conditions in the clause WHERE, you employ an AND operator. To allow that condition to be fulfilled all sides of an condition must be true or the rows won't be displayed.

* Column 1, SELECT,

* SUM(column2)

* FROM "list-of-tables"

* Where "condition1" AND

* "condition2";

The OR operator is also employed to join conditions within the WHERE clause. The different is that both sides of the operator may be true, and the rows can be shown. Both sides or either side will be able to work. For instance:

* SELECT employeeid, firstname, lastname, title, salary

* FROM employee_info

* WHERE the salary is greater than 50000.00 and the title is "Programmer";

In this document we've asked for the employeeid and the firstname, name, the lastname and the salary in instances where the amount is greater than 50000.00 and that the job title is Programer. Both of the conditions must be met to ensure that rows can be displayed. If either one of them are incorrect, the data is not displayed.

Parenthesis can be used around the conditional expressions , if you feel it is easier to read them

* SELECT employeeid, firstname, lastname, title, salary

* FROM employee_info

* Where (salary greater than 50000.00) OR (title is "Programmer");

Another Example:

* SEARCH firstname, lastname salary, title from employee_info Where (title is "Sales") (or (title = "Programmer");

In this particular statement you've requested the firstname as well as the lastname, title and salary . The title is sales and OR programmers. The information comes directly from employee_information table.

IN AND IN BETWEEN

* SECT col 1, SUM(col2)

* FROM "list-of-tables"

* WHERE IS col3

* (list-of-values);

* SECT col1, SUM(col2)

* FROM "list-of-tables"

* WHERE col3 is located between value1 and value3.

* + value2

In the IN conditional operator can be used to test whether the value mentioned prior to the word IN is based on values given after the keyword.

For instance:

* SELECT employeeid, lastname, salary

* FROM employee_info

* WHERE lastname IN ('Hernandez', 'Jones', 'Roberts', 'Ruiz');

In this case in this statement, we're soliciting the employee's ID and last name as well as your salary taken from employee_info tables. We are also requesting to ensure that the lastname is equivalent with Hernandez, Jones, Roberts or Ruiz. The returned rows contain any of those values.

It is also possible to create an IN conditional operator by using compound conditions. This makes use of Equals operator and blends this together with OR and the result is exactly the same

* SELECT employeeid, lastname, salary

* FROM employee_info

* WHERE lastname = 'Hernandez' OR lastname = 'Jones' OR lastname = 'Roberts'

* OR lastname = 'Ruiz';

You can observe in this example as you can see from this example, in this example, the IN operator is much shorter and much more easy to read when it is checked for more than just two values. It is also possible to NOT IN if you would like to exclude specific rows from the table.

We employ BETWEEN to test if the BETWEEN conditional operator whenever we need to verify whether a value declared prior to the word BETWEEN is different from the values that appear immediately after the word.

For instance:

* SELECT employeeid, age, lastname, salary

* FROM employee_info

* WHERE the age is between 30 AND 40

In this statement , we ask for the employee's ID as well as the age, name of the last name and the amount to be taken from the employee_info table in which it is between 30 to 40, and includes the two age ranges. It is also possible to modify this statement without that BETWEEN operator:

* SELECT employeeid, age, lastname, salary

* FROM employee_info

* WHERE AGE > 30 and age 40;

Another use for NOT BETWEEN is when you wish to exclude certain values from your range.

Mathematical Functions

The following basic operators for arithmetic are included in the standard ANSI SQL:

+ Addition

Subtraction

* Multiplication

Division

Modulo is a % Modulo

The modulo operator is used to calculate the rest of division. The modulo operator isn't implemented in ANSI SQL but most databases utilize it and are able to support it. Here are a few other important mathematical functions could be required at some time. These aren't common, so they might not be accessible to you in the relational database management system you're using:

ABS(x) gives the absolute value of x.

SIGN(x) gives the input's sign as -1, 0 or 1 (negative zero, negative or positive)

MOD(x,y) modulo returns the remainder of x multiplied by y (same like x%y)

FLOOR(x) will return the highest integer number that is smaller that or greater than the value of

CEILING(x) (or CEIL(x) yields the lowest integer value more than or greater than x

POWER(x,y) will return the amount of x if it is raised in relation to the value of y.

ROUND(x) Returns the value of the x by the nearest complete number

ROUND(x,d) gives the value of x to the decimal number determined by the value d.

SQRT(x) gives the square-root value for the number x.

For instance:

* SELECT round(salary), firstname

* FROM employee_info

In this letter we've requested the salary figures to be rounded to the nearest total as well as the first name of an employee_info database.

Chapter 9: Outsourcing Of The App Development

Process

If you've got an idea in your head and you're enthusiastic about creating your apps isn't it? But, you'll need money as well as skills and tools to create the application.

Thought about the idea behind your application might be more straightforward than writing the code and then distributing it to mobile users is challenging. Even if you're proficient in the field of software, you will require a trustworthy team of people to complete other duties. Additionally, managing internal staff can be costly. If you don't have the funds to hire one, you might not be able develop and market your app even if it's innovative and well-thought out.

This is where outsourcing comes in to play. When you hire offshore workers to handle the tasks for you you'll be able streamline the development of your application effortlessly. The majority of software development companies have expert computer specialists who will help you create the code for you. You may also consult them further suggestions to improve your work. Furthermore, it'll cost less to contract your entire team.

If you're still skeptical about outsourcing, here are some of the additional benefits you can reap from outsourcing, and some guidelines for selecting the most suitable team.

1. An outsourcing team is driven by results

Outsourcing companies who specialize in the development of software thrive on the feedback they receive from their clients. This is why they're always determined to deliver the highest quality results and meeting your expectations.

2. You'll be in control of the developing phase

Many people are nervous regarding relying on offshore teams because they worry that they won't have a major role to play in the whole production. This isn't the case at all. The outsourcing team is your fingers and toes. Because it's your application they are developing, you have the control over the procedure. You can tell them what you want them to do and they'll begin working to complete your project with a great deal of dedication. Additionally, you are free to take or reject the suggestions of your advisors.

3. You can do more work

Even if you have the majority of the knowledge required to create and market your app, you'll have a difficult time trying to complete all these tasks on your own. When you've got a capable team of experts to assist you it will be simpler to develop your app swiftly. A team is also a way that you'll be able to come up with new ideas. You can have meetings with them so you can enhance the functionality and design of your application. Since they already know how to use the app and procedures, you don't need to show them everything.

4. Cost-efficient

If you're brand new to the field, and you're on the funds to cover it the best option is to you employ an outsourcing company instead of creating an in-house team from the ground up. Naturally, finding team of experts is not going to cost you a penny per dozen. It is, however, cost-effective since you don't have to purchase new equipment or to purchase office space that is good. Companies that outsource already possess the equipment and know-how required to create a great app, and you just have be paying for the services they provide.

However, if your app grows popular and you are able to generate regular streams of revenue and you are able to sustain it, then you might want think about hiring an internal team.

Apart from saving costs, outsourcing can also save you from the stress of managing teams. If there is already a team managerin place, all you have to do is keep track on their activities and then either accept or deny their suggestions. This way, you are able to completely concentrate on making your work better.

Important Tips to Keep in Mind when outsourcing the development of a Software Development Team

It is important to discuss the timeframe and budget with the team. Inform them of the amount of time and money will you be willing to invest for app development. So, they can be able to focus more on their job.

Be specific about your expectations. Do not become one of those stressed customers who don't know what they need. If you would like your team to perform effectively, you must talk to your developers and explain your expectations. Make a plan outlining your objectives and the outcomes that you'd like to achieve. In the beginning of the meeting you should mention all the features you'd like to see in your application. If you have any modifications in mind be sure to notify them as soon as possible.

Be careful. With the rise of tablets and smartphones there are many outsourcing companies available that specialize in creating apps. But, you need be careful when choosing a company to ensure you'll get an outstanding product. Before signing an agreement with a business conduct a bit of study about the company. You might be able to find online reviews or speak to customers who have been their previous customers. It is essential to be aware of the kind of services they provide, the expertise of their staff members, and the prices they charge. Be aware that you are confiding your thoughts to someone else, therefore you must be extremely cautious about the choices you make.

Sign an agreement to not disclose information. You've worked hard in your work Make sure you protect it with care. By signing a non-disclosure contract it is guaranteed that the business will not divulge any details regarding your application.

Be clear with your feedback-If you notice that they are doing something wrong, do not just comment that their work is"ugly"or"dissatisfying."Vague comments like that will only confuse the developers, thus, slowing the production process. To help them improve the quality of their work, you must to be specific in your feedback. Detail each of the positive and negative aspects you observed. Also, be punctual with your replies , so that they can be able to immediately correct any issue.

How do you market your app

With the rise of mobile devices as well as faster internet speeds, an increasing number of people use their devices like smartphones or tablets. This is the reason there are many developers looking to develop applications.

The competition in the market for apps is intense these days. If you're not adept in handling difficult situations, you might not be unable to reach your dream of becoming a successful app creator. To make your app large and stand out from the crowd it is also necessary to devise an effective marketing plan. Remember that there may be other developers that have developed an application with the same idea as your app.

You have to be different from your competition by developing an effective marketing plan. Furthermore, you must be aware of the latest trends in the marketplace. The industry of apps is erratic and constantly evolving. You must constantly alter your strategy to keep up with trends.

Take a look at these powerful marketing strategies that can enable you to stand out your competition.

1. Utilize social media tools

If you want to promote your apps without spending amount of money, you could use various social media platforms like Facebook,

Twitter, Google+, Pinterest, Linkedin and much more.

Social media is a powerful marketing tool as it helps boost the visibility of your business, and can also show its individual aspect. If you can accomplish these things, it's more effective in attracting the correct people-the ones most likely to be attracted to your application.

With an account on social media developers are able to interact with their users live even when they're separated by large distances. Users can also share their opinions about your app which means you can identify areas of your app that need to be further improved.

However, to make use of these platforms effectively you must be aware of the various functions they serve. Pinterest for instance is a popular social media platform to share images; Twitter can be utilized to share updates and news. Google+, on the other hand, is a great option to find people who share the same passion for your product.

2. Form partnerships with advertising networks.

Have you thought about hiring an advertising company to boost the number of users who download your application? It's worth making the move.

If you use your ad-network it is possible to boost your click-through rates by one percent. This may not sound like a lot, but one percent can make you visible in app stores. Additionally, these companies will also help boost your page's ranking in a fair and natural manner.

Ad networks are also aware of the best ways to connect with your intended public using a variety of methods that work.

3. Make use of organic marketing

If you are planning to market your app in different online marketplaces, bear in mind that each market needs a different marketing strategy. This will ensure that your app gets the most exposure and will be able to reach its intended audience.

Have a look at the App Store of Apple. If you want to be successful on this site, you'll have to build a huge number of ads-driven links. However, if you're selling your product through Google Play, you need to attract a large number of people using your product to get higher rankings on their website. A higher number of downloads will result in more traffic, which means that your marketing plan has to be more responsive to the increasing number of notifications from push.

4. Making Loyal Users

Of course, it's not enough to make a significant contribution to brand recognition. A marketing plan will never succeed if you do not create loyal customers.

In order to achieve that, you should provide additional benefits which will make them feel special. Utilizing your app, you can create numerous push notifications that give your users a reward or brand new features. Based on the type of app you create it could be additional weapons and levels for games, or even special discounts and promotions on your products and services.

There are many options to look into. Just remember that you have to ensure that your audience is satisfied with your application.

5. Events

Events let your customers enjoy a more interactive experience with your product. They also get to discover more about your company. If you want to make your event an event that's successful it is essential to provide your guests new services and products which are not available on your application. Perhaps you could hand out some freebiesor invite a well-known band to play during your celebration. Also, you should invite a number of bloggers to promote your event to their followers.

6. Create with a blog

Keep your blog updated regularly with new and interesting articles. If your audience enjoys the content the content they read, they'll be more than happy to share the blog's content via their respective social media channels and increase brand recognition. It is possible to share news about your latest projects, photos videos, articles, and informative content and so much more. But, remember that your content should be relevant to your products and your target audience. A greater amount of content will result in more visitors on your site and application.

Additionally, you remain in contact with bloggers who have the same passion for you. The bloggers have followers of their own. When you've made connections with them, you'll be able also to reach their followers as well. Start by asking users to write reviews on your app, or offer them discounts or freebies.

7. Make a big impression

If you're launching an app that is new to the market, make sure you launch it with a bang. Send out as numerous newsletters to customers as well as bloggers and other people who are important to you. Prior to the date of launch, make sure to post updates and teasers to your website and on social media platforms. If you are connected with the media, you can ask them to provide an early report on the product. Make sure your new product gets the attention of the media.

These are the Best Resources for App Development

The days are gone that you have to be an expert computer engineer to develop an app that is fully functional. Nowadays there are plenty of websites that let users to create a project by starting from beginning to finish. Another benefit of those websites is that they don't have to shell out thousands of dollars, or invest a year or two creating an application. With a modest cost, you'll be able to build, and manage a mobile-friendly website and app. Through these tools, you'll be able to give a better mobile experience for your customers. Here's a comprehensive list of more useful and effective online app creators.

1. Buildfire

If you run small-sized company, this site will make it easy for you to start developing your own mobile application. With Buildfire prospective developers have two options to pick from : you can develop the app yourself or request the site to build it for you for no cost.

If you're looking to take the DIY method, you can simply go to"click and edit. "click then edit" page on the dashboard of the website. Don't worry about it as you do not need to navigate through a maze of codes using this method. Even if you don't have any technical knowledge it is possible to create an application of high-quality in an hour.

Users can use Buildfire's huge collection of colors, content page layouts and much more.

However, if you'd prefer the website to take care of the entire job for you, simply give them the URL for your business's website and your app is up and running within two days. It's always a win-win scenario no matter what option you pick.

Another benefit of this site is their help desk that is able to answer questions. If you have questions you are able to engage with a live chat to talk with one of the U.S.-based personnel. When your app is completed, a representative will be in touch via e-mail or phone.

Buildfire offers free tools for creating an HTML5 online application. You must pay a fee for subscription for creating an app to be used on mobile devices.

2. Como

Formerly named Conduit Mobile Como is a multi-functional app builder that allows its users to develop, market and manage mobile apps they develop.

It is a newly upgraded platform for development, which is called Como Console. Como Console. Like Buildfire it is also possible to use their themes, icons, background designs and designs. You can also include nifty features that will help you effectively manage your business. This includes the ability to process any mobile purchase with MyCheck or track deliveries with Bringg and also purchase items in-app through Online ordering.

In addition to creating your application, you could use Como to manage and distribute the creation. The platform has an online marketing tool called Marketing Genie. It provides numerous options to promote your business both offline and online. Examples include Facebook advertising campaigns including QR codes, stickers and other helpful marketing tools. The site also offers an administration dashboard that tracks how well your application and track user activity, such as reservations, deliveries or in-app purchases, numerous other things.

Como has recently entered into an alliance with Amazon and, as of now, applications you develop are available for Kindle Fire smartphones and tablets. It's free to use however you are able to pay a monthly $33 cost for a premium subscription for access to more features.

3. Mobile Roadie

If you don't own an enterprise, but want to create a mobile application regardless The Mobile Roadie website is definitely the right choice for you. The site lets you develop your own iOS and Android application. It is able to support any media type, and can even upload your work using RSS as well as Google News keyword searches. It also has fans wall, where users can interact with one with one another.

The great thing about Mobile Roadie is that you can preview your app prior to publishing it. This helps you to fix any bugs and errors prior to you publish it to the store. The site will also assist its users in the process of submission. Mobile Roadie will be the one to evaluate the quality and capabilities of your application, ensuring it can be sure that your application will receive positive reviews on the internet.

Utilizing Mobile Roadie, you can take data from various formats like XML, PHP, HTML and even JSON. You can design your own theme and use it across every platform.

To pay the subscription cost you have the option of choosing between the $125 or $667 monthly subscription plan.

4. The App Builder

The name suggests, The App Builder offers various kinds of apps to fulfill the requirements of small and small-sized businesses, employees and even enthusiasts by with two different methods.

Customers can create their apps by themselves using the tools available on the website or leave The App Builder help you in the process.

The site has its own exclusive library, which allows you to modify your apps easily. You can even choose to secure your app using passwords. Additionally, you can update your mobile apps, even after it is live. App Builder is compatible with both Android and Apple devices. App Builder can be used on Apple as well as Android devices.

5. Good Barber

Another website lets you create applications without having to write a long list of code. It offers nine customizable and attractive templates, along with 350 icons and over 600 Google Fonts that you can choose from.

In addition to creating applications that work on Apple or Android devices it is also possible to create websites for absolutely no cost. Your customers are still able to access it via their mobile phones and tablets therefore you can connect with them.

Good Barber regularly sends you notifications when you change the parameters of your product. It also lets you send push notifications to users. To enhance engagement with users, they may post articles, photos and other multimedia on your site.

The site has a annual subscription of $16 or $32. cost.

App Marketplaces

With a variety of platforms for tablets and smartphones being released today, it's not surprising that there are many marketplaces for apps to select from.

In the past, there was only Apple iOS and the Google Play stores. However, now there are additional avenues for developers to explore like Amazon, Windows, and many more.

Each marketplace comes with their own advantages to developers. They also have different payment procedures as well as standards, evaluation charges. It is more likely to be successful if your application is able to be used by a variety of online stores. But, first examine each store. In accordance with their needs it is possible to alter your application in order to conform to their requirements. This chapter will outline the top app stores , as well with other stores you could also look into.

1. iOS App Store

As compared to other marketplaces In comparison to other marketplaces, unlike other app marketplaces, iOS store has more exposure for your product. If your app is evaluated and is accepted by Apple and Apple, your application will stand a good chance of being promoted through different channels like the store's Popular App page, App of the Week page and much more.

If you want to sell your apps through Apple's Apple Store, you will need to pay a fee for registration. But, don't worry about it because it's not too expensive. Additionally, the revenue is also substantial since 70 percent of the revenue goes to the creator. If millions of users install your app and make the in-app purchases you provide, just imagine how much you could get each day.

The process of approval However, the approval process is often quite long. But it's to the benefit of users and the app's developer. Apple stands by the principles of quality and does not want any apps that are mediocre to simply be sold in their stores. They want to ensure that the application you offer has high-quality features and doesn't contain any viruses that are hidden. With their analysis they will allow you to determine the strengths and areas of your product. This could be a challenge for some developers, however when you conduct your homework and develop an original concept, you'll be able to meet Apple's standards.

2. Google Play Store

It is said that the Google Play Store is one of the largest marketplaces for apps. It has more than 700,000 applications and billions of installs each year, you will definitely make plenty of income and loyal users on this site. In contrast to those who use the iOS App Store, the submission process isn't so difficult. Furthermore, he is more able to alter and modify the look and feel of the application.

When your app is live and available on Google Play Store, you can begin to build your own client base and help make your business more profitable by selling your app. Of course, you'll have to create a quality application to get the respect and admiration of the people you want to attract.

Google Play requires you to pay a fee of $25 for the initial registration cost. The low cost makes it an ideal opportunity for budding developers who don't have much money. The only issue you'll face will be that Android's Android OS is extremely dispersed. It means that there may be a few variations based on the device you are using. The app could function on one smartphone however, it might not function correctly on a tablet of a different brand.

3. Amazon

Amazon is among the latest marketplaces for apps that has opened its doors. Customers who have Kindle devices will visit the store to buy new applications. Beware of the name since Amazon isn't just about shopping or reading apps. Apps for entertainment can also flourish in this market. Furthermore, Kindle devices are also increasing in popular, therefore it should be beneficial to branch into this market.

The first thing to note is that it is important to note that the Amazon App Store only has more than 50,000 applications in its list. This means the competition isn't yet very fierce. A new idea could excel in this market since every app is easily recognizable for other customers. Additionally, Amazon also allows some of their apps to run for Android devices. This can result in greater profits in the long term.

Amazon also offers an interesting feature that assists customers with their purchasing choices. If a user browses the merchandise on Amazon the site, it will show products that match the items he or she is purchasing. It's a simple strategy that will increase the number of downloads and eyes.

Amazon also has an online payment system that makes it simple to buy applications. In addition to providing support for customers, they have a team of experts who assists developers. If you have questions regarding their approval process or fees for registration, you can simply talk to a member of their representatives.

4. Windows

Prior to that, Windows only caters to laptops and desktop computers. However, as the demands for mobile devices grows it is now producing applications that are specifically designed for tablets and smartphones. Like Amazon and Amazon, it is the case that Windows app store has only a handful of apps. With just 120,000 applications this makes it much easier for your app to be noticed by other users. The process of evaluating apps is swift and easy since they are still trying to draw a large number of developers. However, this does not mean they will not accept badly-designed applications.

Additionally, you can even create apps for computers, giving an additional avenue to market your brand. If you do not have the resources to build your application and you need help, we are eager to give you assistance in the development of your app.

The latest Windows Phone 8 devices also come with a brand unique option called"lock screen spotlight."This useful feature will display the top apps that users typically use, and other recommended apps that relate to what they've recently downloaded. This feature will assist struggling developers to increase their visibility.

Chapter 10: The Qualities Of A Good App

Many people regularly download a variety of applications. The problem is that they may not make use of every app they download for their tablets and smartphones. If, for instance, you have 50 apps installed in their devices, there's an excellent likelihood that they'll only use the majority of the apps. They might try your application for a few days, but after they become bored or have found an alternative that's superior, they'll quit using it. The worst part is that they'll uninstall your application so they can download another.

This is the reality of the world of app development. If you believed that gaining their attention is difficult to achieve, you could face many difficulties in meeting their ever-growing demands.

This is the reason you have to create your app which is appealing and practical. It must be easy to access and simple to use, to ensure that users will not get frustrated by your app. Additionally, it should also contain lots of content, to ensure that users don't be bored.

Here are a few characteristics you should be looking for when creating a successful application.

1. Stable

Before you can launch your app on the market place it must pass rigorous testing and simulations. Examine your app to determine and see if it works in extreme conditions. Then you will be able to understand what your application's comprised of.

Of course, it's impossible for your invention to perform in every scenario. If you create an online gaming application for instance you can't be sure that it will work when there isn't an internet connection. The app must go through thorough testing to ensure that you are able to resolve any issues. It's embarrassing if your customers were the first one to find a flaw in your app and you don't know what to do to solve it.

To create an application that is more reliable be sure it doesn't consume many system resources. If, for instance, your mobile platform can run background applications, be sure that your app doesn't consume much battery life, memory, or CPU power to ensure that it remains in the mobile device of the user.

2. User Interface

If people view your application in the online store the first thing they'll notice is its general appearance. After they have installed your program you will be in a position to gain a better perception of the app's user interface.

If your app doesn't appear attractive to your intended audience or if the navigation controls aren't that fluid, users will definitely delete that application from their mobile devices.

Be aware that your users use devices with tiny screens. Therefore, as much as is possible your user interface should not be cluttered with many obstructions. The best applications are those which do not contain lots of buttons or design elements that are not needed.

3. Be able to meet the demands of your customers

The process of creating an app is simpler than advertising and managing. At times the app's developers typically inform their users of an imminent system update. These updates enable tech experts to update the content or fix any glitches or bugs.

Although your app costs $99 however, you must give them plenty of features that are worth it for you to ensure they remain faithful to your brand.

Check out the most popular game on mobile known as Angry Birds. The highly addictive game has just recently celebrated the 250 millionth download. In addition to having an original gameplay one of the reasons Angry Birds became immensely popular is the fact that the creators constantly upgrade their game with special events, products or new levels, and many more.

Today, there are more than five variations of Angry Birds on the market. This means that people who were enthralled by the first game previously have brand the chance to discover new realms.

4. Convenience

This is yet another crucial quality you must include in your application. Can users navigate your application with only one hand? Does your application have custom features that will enhance the user experience? Does it run without an internet connection?

Learn about your target market in depth. Find their issues and evaluate their needs by using your application. In addition to a smooth navigation system and an easy user interface, having quality and useful content is a useful feature.

5. Security

If your application requires customers to disclose certain personal details What can you do to ensure their security offline and online? The information they transmit to you should be secured by a robust security system. If your mobile application syncs data with its counterpart on the internet it is essential to enhance the security on the internet to ensure nobody can access their private information.

6. Personalization

Your users should be able customize your app to their preferences and needs. Offer them flexible options so that they are able to alter certain aspects of your application. This does not only address personalizing content. It also involves gaining an understanding of the information that they save and share or even use.

7. The load is loaded quickly.

The majority of mobile users are not able to pay attention and therefore it is a good idea to create apps that load in a matter of seconds. Of course, apps that are entertainment-oriented are bound to take longer to load because of the data they have to process.

If your app is one of the social media or camera application, the loading time should be quick.

8. Non-intrusive Advertising

Aren't you annoyed when a pop-up advertisement pops up on your computer's screen? It's okay to put advertisements on your application. However, you must ensure that they're not intrusive and distracting. Graphic overlays and banner ads must be minimal to ensure that they do not consume enough space on your screen. It is also recommended to display these ads while the application is in the process of loading.

Helpful Tips to Create Your App

With the abundance of digital and traditional tools developing apps has become a breeze for anyone. If you're a novice designer, budding entrepreneur or someone who doesn't have the technical skills it is easy to make money from web-based and mobile applications providing you have the proper tools.

But, creating a popular app that people will often use is a completely different ballgame. If you're hoping to make your app exceptional, you must be exceptional in your own way. You must have the ability to predict the next big trend, an sense of new ideas and a burning drive to achieve.

It requires years of experience and hard work to develop these abilities. The book's pages might not be sufficient to go over all the elements that you have to do be able to do to become an experienced developer and business owner. But, this chapter will provide you with some of the basics that you should be aware of in order to make an app that is successful. It's a small piece of information however it will aid you on your long road to victory. Learn these tips below.

1. Learn to speak the language of your user

Be aware that you create an application to make connections with your customers and to improve their quality of life. In order to connect towards them, you must be able to comprehend your audience, as well as potential customers as well. Discover their lifestyle. Learn about the things they search for on the internet and study their mobile usage habits. What is the average amount of time they spend on the internet? What other apps do they use that they use most often?

When you are aware of these aspects when you understand these concepts, it will become simpler to create an app that is effective for users.

2. Don't forget to include options that can also function offline.

A lot of users are online for long periods of time doesn't mean you shouldn't add online functions. There are many applications that have been successful have received praise for their performance due to their ability to function even when users aren't connected to the internet. Digital apps for mobile such as Pocket, WorkFlowy, and even Evernote are able to function flawlessly even when the user is not connected to the WiFi hotspot.

This idea must be taken into consideration when you and your development team start creating an application. With offline capabilities it is possible to assure that your users will continue to find your application useful even if they're not connected to an internet connection.

3. Make it simple and simple to utilize

Save your users from complex online registrations, highly technical user interfaces and non-responsive navigational buttons. Do not assume that your audience is an expert. Simply because everyone is are using a tablet or smartphone doesn't mean they're experts on their devices. You must ensure that even beginners with mobile devices are able to quickly navigate through your applications.

To determine if your project is easy enough for ordinary people to comprehend, search for someone in your family or a colleague who isn't tech-savvy and then let them test your application. What do they think of when using the app? Do they shake their heads when they hit the button? Are they complaining that directions are hard to comprehend? Pay attention to areas they find difficult to navigate. Many new users uninstall an application if they think that the layout isn't intuitive enoughor is too complicated to navigate.

4. Be aware that one size may not fit all.

One of the biggest errors that novice developers make is to not tailor their apps upon the device or operating system. Windows, Apple, and Android users use different methods of installing and making use of apps. Additionally the size of the screen is a major factor in the procedure.

You must ensure that you have multiple versions of your program to ensure it can meet the diverse needs of every operating system.

5. Start your app on different platforms

Of course, more platforms equal increased users. The modern technophile typically uses their apps from a variety of devices and platforms. They may open it on computers or tablet, as well as on websites and mobile phones. Be sure your app is universal. But, the style as well as the functionality and aesthetics will be the same across all platform.

6. Emulate real life experiences

Another important aspect in making a great app is its capacity to replicate real-life experiences. If, for instance, you're creating an app focused on helping users be successful in their studies, then you must be looking into how they complete their assignments in the real world. You could use physical items and ask them questions about their habits of studying. When you have a clear understanding of the situation, you can find an opportunity to make your app will enhance the experience of users. For instance, if it's a study app, perhaps you could add an option that allows them to note down notes, or save research material in their phones.

7. Be an expert in one thing

Another common error that novice developers make is to add too many features to their apps. Being an expert in every field is a huge problem because it makes your app difficult to understand. It doesn't matter whether your application serves one purpose, so long as it does it well. When designing your app make sure you are precise and specific about what it will and should not accomplish. Don't assume that if you present many options at your users, they'll be able to choose the best option after a certain time. Instead, point them to the specific experience you would like your users to experience.

8. Monitor user feedback

Go through your website and social media channels each and every now and then to observe how your users react to your application. Their feedback can help you analyze your work and identify any issues or areas that require to be addressed quickly. Of course, you need to be aware that not every post on your wall on Facebook can be helpful. Learn to distinguish the comments that are trolls from constructive criticisms to ensure that your application will be improved.

Chapter 11: Methods And Classes

As you get started in Swift then you'll create methods and classes frequently, therefore let's look at the basics of how they function. Clear out all the junk you have within your playground file. you need a clean slate to begin working on. This is the moment you can begin creating your first app. It's an app called a Tip Calculator. This app will be developed each piece of code each step and I'll discuss each component as we build it. Ready? In your playfile:

* // 1

* class TipCalculator {* class TipCalculator

* }

The first thing you're creating a class. To create it, simply enter class and then begin by putting in the name which is, in this instance, TipCalculator. Then, follow this by using curly braces.

Within the curly braces enter this code:

* // 2

* Let total double

* Allow taxPct double

* Subtotals Double

114

There will be some errors appear as you type in this code, but don't fret about them. They will be rectified in time. What you've done is to define properties on the class, exactly the same way as you create variables or constants. There are three properties that you've created that include the total amount of the bill prior to when tax is added the tax percentage that is included and the total amount of the bill prior to the tax has been added.

The reason why you're experiencing errors at this point is due to the fact that you have to declare properties that have an initial value. We did not do that in this instance.

In continuation of the code you've just entered, you can add these lines, keeping within these curly braces

* // 3

* init(total: Double, taxPct: Double) {

* self.total = total

* self.taxPct = taxPct

* subtotal = total / (taxPct + 1)

* }

This is the process that creates the initializer of the class, and they are named init within Swift. The initializer is comprised of two parameters.

Since they have the identical name, they can be distinct by the addition of the prefix self.

If you're staying within those curly braces, you can add this in your own code

```
* // 4

*  func  calcTipWithTipPct(tipPct:  Double)  ->
Double {

* Return Subtotal * tipPct

* }
```

This is where you use the func keyword to create an operation that is followed by parameters. Here you have to be clear with the types, and then you complete it by returning the type. It is a very simple function that increases the bill's subtotal in the amount of the tip. Following that you can add the following code:

```
* // 5

* func printPossibleTips() {

* println("15%: \(calcTipWithTipPct(0.15))")

* println("18%: \(calcTipWithTipPct(0.18))")

* println("20%: \(calcTipWithTipPct(0.20))")
```

You've developed a new method that prints three possible tips. Be aware that when a method is invoked within the instance in a class the first parameter doesn't require to be named, however the other ones do. Then, you can add the code above, but this time, following that curly brace:

* // 6

* let tipCalc = TipCalculator(total: 33.25, taxPct: 0.06)

* tipCalc.printPossibleTips()

In the last step you've created an account for the tooltip calculator. Then, you've used the method that will show possible values for tips.

This is the way is the ideal code for you to look right now:

* // 1

* class TipCalculator {* class TipCalculator

* // 2

* Let Total * let total

* Allow taxPct Double

* Let subtotal Double

* // 3

* init(total: Double, taxPct: Double) {

* self.total = total

* self.taxPct = taxPct

* subtotal = total / (taxPct + 1)

* }

* // 4

*   func   calcTipWithTipPct(tipPct: Double)   ->
Double {

* Return subtotal * tipPct

* }

* // 5

* func printPossibleTips() {

* println("15%: \(calcTipWithTipPct(0.15))")

* println("18%: \(calcTipWithTipPct(0.18))")

* println("20%: \(calcTipWithTipPct(0.20))")

* }

* }

* // 6

* let tipCalc = TipCalculator(total: 33.25, taxPct:
0.06)

* tipCalc.printPossibleTips()

Arrays and Loops. Loops

There's probably some duplicates in the code
above. This is because you've used the method
calcTipWithTotal multiple times, with various

percentages. This is the place where arrays can help and help reduce the amount of duplication.

You can go to the place where you written printPossibleTips. Replace the text by:

* Let the possibility of possibleTipsInferred equal [0.15, 0.18, 0.20* let possibleTipsInferred = [0.15, 0.18, 0.20

* let possibleTipsExplicit:[Double] = [0.15, 0.18, 0.20]

* You've constructed an assortment of doubles making use of both explicit and inferred typing. Add the following lines below that:

* for possibleTip {in possibleTipsInferred from possibleTipsInferred

*   println("\(possibleTip*100)%: \(calcTipWithTipPct(possibleTip))")

* }

Dictionaries

We'll make one last modification to your code. Rather than just displaying your tips in print, you could instead make a dictionary which has all the data.

You've reached the point where you written printPossibleTips, and then erase the method. Replace it by:

* // 1

* func returnPossibleTips() -> [Int: Double] {

* Let potentialTipsInferred be [0.15, 0.18, 0.20* let possibleTipsInferred = [0.15, 0.18, 0.20

* let possibleTipsExplicit:[Double] = [0.15, 0.18, 0.20]

* // 2

* var Retval = [Int Double()()

* for {possibleTip in possibleTipsInferred possible tip in possibleTipsInferred

* let intPct = Int(possibleTip*100)

* // 3

* retval[intPct] = calcTipWithTipPct(possibleTip)

* }

* Retval return

* }

You will be able to see an error, but we'll correct this right now. You must edit the last line in your file to be read as:

* tipCalc.returnPossibleTips()

Congratulations! You've just created your initial class using Swift!

120

Creating Your First iOS App

After you've mastered the fundamentals of Swift programming and developed the Tip Calculator class and then learn how to build your first iOS application. We'll use this Tip Calculator class that you designed and develop an interface for the user.

Getting Started

* Gt Xcode opened and was able to open

* File\New\Project

* Choose iOS\Application\Single View Application

* Click Next

* When it asks you for the product's name Enter TipCalculator

• Set the Language to Swift

* Set devices to iPhone

Make sure that the checkbox on the right side of Use Core Data is not marked

* Click Next to continue.

Select the directory to which you'd like to save your project, then click Create

Now let's review of what Xcode can do for you. On the left-hand side of Xcode Click on iPhone 6 Simulator and then play. There should be an

Xcode splash screen with the words Tip Calculator and after that, a blank screen should show up. It is now time filling the blank screen!

Designing Your Model

Before we can begin developing the user interface we must create an app model. It is basically a collection of classes that is representative of the information in your app, as well as the actions the app will to execute upon the collected data.

To be used in this tutorial your model will comprise the TipCalculator class you created in the playground , but you will change its name to TipCalculatorModel.

To include this class, click on the open

* File\New\File

* Choose iOSSourceSwift File

* Call it TipCalculatorModel.swift,

"Click" on "Create."

What you'll need to do is transfer your playground file into an easy file as it's not possible to access the code contained within a playground file. they are only to be used for testing.

Open TipCalculator.swift

Copy the class you have created from your play file (not the test lines at the lower) in the Swift file and then make these modifications

Change the name of your class TipCalculatorModel

You will need to alter the taxPct and total to variables

It is necessary to convert subtotal property to a computed one and do this by substituting the subtotal property using this code

* {var subtotal: Double Variant subtotal: Double

* get {

* return total / (taxPct + 1)

* }

* }

Computed properties don't save the values they store, but they are computed using other values. In this case, you will be computing the subtotal each time it is requested, based on the total and taxPct.

Then, you must eliminate the entire line which set the subtotal value in init, and also remove any comments contained in the file.

Once you've finished your work, it will look something like:

* //

* // TipCalculatorModel.swift

* /*/ TipCalculator

* //

* /Created by Main Account on 12/18/14.

* Copyright (c) 2014 Razeware LLC. Copyright (c) 2014 Razeware LLC. All rights reserved.

* //

* import Foundation

* class TipCalculatorModel {

* var total: Double

* Variant taxPct Double

* {var subtotal: Double Variant Subtotal: Double

* get {

* return total / (taxPct + 1)

* }

* }

* init(total: Double, taxPct: Double) {

* self.total = total

* self.taxPct = taxPct

* }

```
* func  calcTipWithTipPct(tipPct:  Double)  ->
Double {

* Return Subtotal * tipPct

* }

* func returnPossibleTips() -> [Int: Double] {

* Let potentialTipsInferred be [0.15, 0.18, 0.20*
Let possibleTipsInferred = [0.15, 0,18, 0.20

* let  possibleTipsExplicit:[Double]  =  [0.15,  0.18,
0.20]

* var the retval value = [Int Double()()

*   for  {possibleTip  in  possibleTipsInferred
possibleTip from possibleTipsInferred

* let intPct = Int(possibleTip*100)

* retval[intPct] = calcTipWithTipPct(possibleTip)

* }

* Retval return

* }

* }
```

Once your app model is finished now is the time
to take a examine the view!

Chapter 12: An Introduction To Storyboards And

The Interface Builder

The user interface for your app is going be built using a tool known as a Storyboard and Xcode incorporates Interface Builder, a neat tool that allows you to easily modify Storyboards. Interface Builder allows you to create all the controls - labels, buttons text fields, buttons and the rest of the controls within your application by dropping and dragging. These are known as Views. Check the left part of Xcode and select Main.storyboard. This will display the interface builders. It is very detailed, so we will only cover one area of the screen at a time:

The left side on the left Project Navigator - where your project files are displayed.

To the left of the Interface Builder is the Document Outline Your views will be viewed in a single glance on every screen of your app . Make sure that you click the down arrows below the items to view the whole document.

Your application has only one view controller. However, we'll be adding more functionality to it very soon.

If you look to the left of the view controller and you will see an Arrow. This view controller is your

Initial View Controller - this is the first screen that is displayed when the app launches. It is possible to change this using the drag arrow towards an alternative view controller.

If you look at the lower part in the Interface Builder You will notice some terms "w Any" and "h Any". This means that your app has been edited to run on any size of interface.

On the top in the top of the View Controller there are three small icons . which are the controller First Responder, Exit and Controller. There is no need to be concerned about them for the sake of this guide.

Take a look at the bottom left side of Interface Builder, and you'll see four icons connected with Auto Layout - again, you won't be using these in this tutorial.

On the right-hand part on the right hand side of Interface Builder there are Inspectors that are used to display what's been specified in the Outline. Outline. There are a variety of tabs. You will be making use of these during this instructional.

Not to be left out at the bottom on the Interface Builder is the Libraries. They list the various types of view controllers you can include in your application.

Making your Views

If you're a bit rusty the class TipCalculatorModel, it contains two inputs: the tax percentage as well as an amount. The best thing for users of your application is to enter the total using your numeric keyboards on the iPhone This is where a text input field can be useful. Since taxes are typically limited to a small of a certain range, you'll need the slider.

In addition to both the text fields and slider, you'll require an appropriate label for each and a button to perform the calculation and a bar that displays your name and the title of the application and a text field which shows the results.

If you're prepared to begin building the user interface of your app, piece by piece each step:

1. Navigation Bar Instead of directly adding it, go to the outline of the document and then select View Controller. Then go to EditorEmbed inNavigation Controller. This creates an navigation bar within your view controller. Double click it and enter the text in tip Calculator.

2. Labels - go to the Object Library and add a label to the control panel view. Double click the label , and place the text in the form of Bill total (Post-Tax):.. Now select the label and click the fifth tab in the Inspectors section. This will be the Size Inspector. Set it to X=33, and it's Y=81. The same

procedure can be applied to another label, but with the text set to tax percentage (0 %):, X=20, and Y=120.

3. Text Field - visit the Object Library and drag a text field onto the controller for view. Select the Attribute Inspector, and then set the keyboard type to Decimal Pad. Select the Size Inspector, and set the values X=192, Y=77 and Width=392.

4. Slider - Visit the Object Factory, and slide a slider into the object, afterwards go into the Attribute Inspector and set the Minimum Value to 0 10 and Maximum Value = 10. the current value to 6. Then , go in the Size inspector and change X=190,Y=116, and Width=396

5. Button - Go back to Object Library Drag a button into. Double-click it to place the text in Calculate , and then change your Size Inspector for X=268 with Y=154.

6. Text View Text View: Drag a Text View out of the Objects Library and then double click on it , and then remove the text there. Visit the Attributes Inspector and make sure Editable and Selectable haven't been verified. Visit the Size Inspector and select the following values: X=16; Y=192; Width=5 and the height to 400.

7. Tap Gesture Recognizer Return to Object Library and drag in the Tap to Gesture Recognizer

to the main view. This will inform the user when they tap the view to turn off the keyboard.

8. Auto-Layout Interface Builder is a great tool for creating a high-quality auto-layout constraint. To accomplish this, open the Document Outline and select Main View. Click the third button on the lower right corner in the Interface Builder and choose Add Missing constraints.

Now you can create the app and then run it through your iPhone 6 Simulator and you will be able to see the fundamental user interface!

A View Controller Tour

Okay, you've created an app model , and the views for your app, so you can look at the controller for views.

Open ViewController.swift. This will display the code that controls your view controller or screen, inside the application. This is the component that manages the communication between the model and the views. If you look at the class, you will find this code

* // 1

* Import UIKit

* // 2

* class ViewController: UIViewController {

* // 3

* override func viewDidLoad() {

* super.viewDidLoad()

* // Perform any additional configuration after loading the view with an ipad.

* }

* // 4

* override func didReceiveMemoryWarning() {

* super.didReceiveMemoryWarning()

* // Get rid of any resources that could be duplicated.

* }

* }

In the next section, you'll find a few parts of code which you're not familiar with. Let's examine them one by one:

iOS is divided into several frameworks. Each one has distinct codes. Before you can access the code of a framework you have to import it. The framework that includes the base class used for view controllers is known as UIKit and also includes buttons, text fields and much more. For the very first time that you've seen an example of subclasses. Now you're creating a new class called

ViewController which is a subclass of UIViewController. To learn how this is done change the declaration of the class by:

* class UIViewController {

* }

You can see that UIKit.UIViewController is referring to UIViewController class in the namespace for UIKit.

The Override method works by using a root view of the controller at first accessing it. If you want to override an algorithm, you need to make use of the override keyword to ensure that you don't override an error-prone method.

It is the Memory Function method is called when the iPhone is running low in memory.

Linking the View Controller with your Views

If you've got a basic understanding regarding the View Controller class you need to add properties to the sub views and then add them into the Interface Builder. To do this, visit your ViewController's class, search for viewDidLoad and add the following code prior to that:

* @IBOutlet var totalTextField : UITextField!

* @IBOutlet var taxPctSlider : UISlider!

* @IBOutlet var taxPctLabel : UILabel!

* @IBOutlet var resultsTextView : UITextView!

You are declaring four different variables:

* UITextField

* UISlider

* UILabel

* UITextView

There are two differences between this and how you created the file from the playground:

The prefix for the variables in question is called @IBoutLet. Interface Builder will go through your code to find these variables, and this is what lets you connect these variable to your views.

Every Variable is marked with an! to signal that they are not required values, but are unwrapped implicitly. This is a nice way to say the code you write is created in a way that it is set and, in the event that it's not set, the app will crash.

Let's take a look at linking these elements to the components of our user interface.

* Open Main.storyboard

* Choose the view controller for Document Outline

* Open Connections Inspector - tab number 6

Below you'll find the properties you previously created that are which are listed in Outlets.

Go to the right side of the resultsTextView and you'll see a tiny circle. Press CTRL and drag this button onto it's Text View, which is located under the button to calculate. When you release the mouse, your property is joined to the text view.

Make sure to do this for all the properties, ensuring that each property is connected to the right element.

Connecting your Actions with your View Controller

We will link actions with methods in order to:

Switch on ViewController.swift

Include the following code in any place in the class:

* @IBAction func calculateTapped(sender : AnyObject) {

* }

* @IBAction func taxPercentageChanged(sender : AnyObject) {

* }

* @IBAction function viewTapped(sender anyObject) {•

* }

The signature must be used whenever you create an action callback from views. The signature is essentially an undefined function with no return value. It takes one parameter that is of type AnyObject. it is the class of any kind.

In order to ensure you are sure that Interface Builder has spotted the new methods you have added and they need to be marked with the word @IBAction.

Go again to Main.storyboard and make sure whether your view controller is selected in the Document Outline. Verify that the 6th tab, called Connections Inspector is opened and then look into the section titled Received Actions. your new method will be displayed in that section.

Check the right side of the calculateTapped and locate the circle. Drag from that circle until the button labeled calculate. A pop-up screen will be displayed and you can choose to the option to Touch Up Inside. When you do this, you're stating you are saying that "when the user removes their finger off the screen after touching the button, use my calculation method:".

Repeat the same procedure for the remaining methods , and make sure they are in the correct locations:

taxPercentageChanged has to be dragged onto the slider, and connected to the value that has changed - this section will be called when the user taps the slider within the application

viewTapped needs to be dragged in order to the Tap Gesture Recognizer located in Document Outline. It is not necessary to choose a gesture to use to use this feature.

Connecting your View Controller your Model

You're almost done building your first iOS application. All you have to do is connect the view controller with your model.

ViewController.swift ViewController.swift

Include the following code in your class. It will provide a means to refresh the interface

* let tipCalc = TipCalculatorModel(total: 33.25, taxPct: 0.06)

* func refreshUI() {

* // 1

* totalTextField.text = String(format: "%0.2f", tipCalc.total)

* // 2

* taxPctSlider.value = Float(tipCalc.taxPct) * 100.0

* // 3

* taxPctLabel.text = "Tax Percentage (\(Int(taxPctSlider.value))%)"

* // 4

* resultsTextView.text = ""

* }

Include a refreshUI call beneath viewDidLoad

* refreshUI()

* Implement taxPercentageChanged and viewTapp using this code

* @IBAction func taxPercentageChanged(sender : AnyObject) {

* tipCalc.taxPct = Double(taxPctSlider.value) / 100.0

* refreshUI()

* }

* @IBAction function viewTapped(sender the object: anyObject) {•

* totalTextField.resignFirstResponder()

* }

Finally, implement calculateTapped using this code:

* @IBAction func calculateTapped(sender : AnyObject) {

* // 1

* tipCalc.total = Double((totalTextField.text as NSString).doubleValue)

* // 2

* let possibleTips = tipCalc.returnPossibleTips()

*var outcomes = ""

* // 3

* for (tipPct and tipsValue) in possibleTips{

* // 4

* results + "\(tipPct) percent: \(tipValue)\n"

* }

* // 5

* resultsTextView.text = results

Your app is now complete Simply create it, launch it, and rejoice in knowing that you created it!

Chapter 13: Making The Ios App With Swift -

Advanced

The app you created in the previous chapter was a simple tip calculator that was designed to provide you with some idea on how you can navigate Swift. We're going to create something more complicated and complicated. Follow each step as described below and you'll successfully create a complete iOS app using Swift.

What You Are Looking For

*A Mac computer that has Mavericks or Yosemite installed

* Xcode 6

* An understanding of Swift and Swift, which you ought to have mastered by the end of this text.

Getting Started

In the previous chapter I explained the steps to set up Xcode and Xcode, so go through the same steps. Once it's fully installed and configured it is time to start Xcode and start a brand new project by pressing shift+cmd+N.

You can go there to go through go to the Template Selector and verify that iOSApp has been picked.

Choose the template that you want to use. Master-Detail Application.

This template is a fantastic starting point since it has the storyboard setup with everything you'll require. The template also includes an appropriate controller for both the Detail controller as well as the Master controller. The reason we're choosing this particular template that you'll be creating an app for task lists.

Once you've chosen your Master Detail Application template, select Next to move onto the next step of the setup.

In the next screen you will be able to see the wizard to set up your project and you'll need to fill in a few fields and select a few alternatives.

The first step is to name your application. Enter the name in the name field of the app. You can name it however you want so long as you can remember it. However, for purpose of the tutorial I'm calling it TaskMe.

Next step, you must fill out your Organization Name field correctly and follow up with step 3: Organization Identifier field. This is where you'll need an reverse domain name to identify the.

It is the Organization Identifier is going to aid you in creating the Bundle Identifier. It gives your application an unique name and is applicable to Apple and all the iOS devices.

Select and click Language and then, using the drop-down menu, make sure that Swift is selected instead of Objective C. In this way it will ensure that the majority of the code Xcode creates will be produced in Swift files, and not those created specifically for Objective C.

The final step is to select Devices and then from the drop-down menu, select iPhone. Verify that the option to use Core Data isn't selected. Although Core Data is great to study, we don't require it for this tutorial.

Learning through Experimentation

Before we begin creating custom code, I'd like to briefly look at what you could discover from this code created using Xcode following the selection of to use the Master Detail Application template. It is already a functioning application, therefore you need to create and test it to see the possibilities it has using cmd+R.

If you try playing around with it, you'll be able to see the List screen that has the + and edit button in your navigation bar. Click + in order to include a row to the list. The list will display the date and the time it was added. If you click or tap on the row, you'll get a detail screen that displays the date and data at the center. In the list screen, you can remove rows using two ways by either tapping them with a swipe and pressing Delete, or clicking Edit and then delete them from there.

Now, before we move forward, let's take another glance at the code that has been created by Xcode.

AppDelegate.swift

The base for your app is an application named AppDelegate.swift Let's take a look at the source code it includes. Do not pay attention to the notes appear on the front of the file, and then go to the very first section of code. The code should be a proper read

* Import UIKit into

This code will enable you to gain access to everything that is offered within UIKit. If you've ever done programming using Objective C, then you'll discover this to be very familiar, but contrary to Objective C, you'll import a whole module instead of just header files specific to a structure or class. It is a common practice practically every single file in the application, regardless of whether it's for UIKit or the more basic Foundation files.

The next code line, it appears a bit odd:

* @UIApplicationMain

In Swift you'll notice that there is no mail file, as there is in other programming languages. In fact, when creating for an iOS application, you'll be required to point Xcode to the particular file you would like to consider as the principal file. This can be done by adding this attribute to an Swift class. It is extremely unlikely that you'll even be able to change the location from which Xcode finds it, but it's a good idea to understand exactly what this nebulous piece of code is doing.

We now have a definition of a class that is used in AppDelegate. AppDelegate file. If you look at it, you will see that it inherits from UIResponder and from the UIApplicationDelegate protocol. If you're familiar with programming Objective C, you'll be able to see the syntax as a huge improvement over how we were using it.

* class AppDelegate: UIResponder, UIApplicationDelegate {

Take a look at how the AppDelegate class is implemented and you'll see that there's very nothing happening here. You're left with an empty window variable as well as many functions that are unfilled or contain very few information in their implementation.

In reality, the only function with executable code is

* application:didFinishingLaunchingWithOptions:

All that's happening is returning to the true

* func application(application: UIApplication, didFinishLaunchingWithOptions launchOptions: [NSObject: AnyObject]?) >> Bool {* func application(application: UIApplication, didFinishLaun

* // Use this Point for modification after launch of application.

* Return true

* }

What's going on? And the reason for why this application has not stopped working is due to some hidden magic. If you peek at the setting of your application, you'll notice that the launching point has been set to Main.storyboard and is responsible to set up the window and controllers that will be activated when the application starts.

The only other part of code that's worthy of mentioning in this moment is the definition of variables to define the windows:

* Variable Window: UIWindow?

This will be the one responsible for creating a variable property within AppDelegate as well as the help of a UIWindow that is not required in its nature. It is stated in the same way, as you can see in the above example, as UIWindow? Take note of the question mark at the end of the code.

If you've not yet learned something about options The idea behind them is that they're the only ones that can have anything or nothing, i.e. have a value of nil. You don't have to know much about them in this guide however, if you plan to use Cocoa Touch Framework, you should know that. Cocoa Touch Framework.

One thing to be aware of about options and this is how they are employed in the parameter types. You'll notice that certain types in Swift have an exclamation mark. This is known is an explicit unwrapped, optional

* @IBOutlet weak var detailDescriptionLabel: UILabel!

The distinction between an ordinary option and an optional that is implicitly wrapped is that, if attempt using the former even though there is no value, you'll receive an error at runtime, just as if you tried to remove a normal optional and then use it without value. This is why they are only used that are extremely likely that there will have an equivalent value. If there was any value, it could result in a major error.

You might also have noticed in the parameter's second section that it is made up of two names

* application:didFinishLaunchingWithOptions:

The first name is didFinishLaunchingWith0ptions and, when the function is called, this acts as the public name. The second name is launch0ptions , and is being the title of the constant whenever it is utilized within the parameters of the specific function.

* func application(application: UIApplication, didFinishLaunchingWithOptions launchOptions: [NSObject: AnyObject]?) >> Bool {* func application(application: UIApplication, didFinishLaun

MasterViewController.swift

If you look at the file, you'll discover that there's plenty of information within the file. You have already seen import in AppDelegate and you may already have figured out that MasterViewController class inherits from UITableViewController. I will not go through each tiny bit of code but only the ones that are intriguing because they offer significant enhancements when compared to how this could be executed using Objective C.

In a short look at this code there's one other feature that stands out: the term "override" and the way it was used in the past for practically every task:

* override func awakeFromNib() {

* override func viewDidLoad() {

* override func didReceiveMemoryWarning() {

A majority function names have were defined within the MasterViewController superclass or in some other part of the chain of ancestry. therefore, you need to clearly inform the compiler you'd like to extend or override the functions that are already available inside the function of ancestor. This can cut down the chance of making mistakes in the event that you choose to use an unintentional function name that has been utilized elsewhere. If you were to do this, then everything could break.

So, looking at the MasterViewController, you can see the first part is the objects variable property definition, which has been initialized using the empty NSMutableArray()

* Vari objects = NSMutableArray()

Once the view on your controller has finished loading the viewDidLoad method will be invoked. The method will start using the Superclass method. you'll soon be able to observe how this works in almost all functions similar to this.

147

The superclass calls are followed by the left and right bar buttons being set up. The thing to be noted is the usage of addButton which is an ongoing feature. This is recommended for the other similar items which will never change after having been designed. Another aspect that is interesting is UIBarButtonItem being created:

* UIBarButtonItem(barButtonSystemItem: .Add, target: self, action: "insertNewObject:")

Instead of the voluminous syntax of Objective C, in which you call alloc, and then initWithWhatever, Swift does away from that and makes use of named arguments instead in the initializer.

You should also note that the way we tell it the type of UIBarButtonSystemItem we want to use is much nicer. Instead of typing UIBarButtonSystemAdd, instead you can just use. Add. This is possible due to Swift's ability infer the type of a thing it simply picks the type of work you're doing and figure out the proper kind automatically.

Check out insertNewObject and you'll be able to see an interesting type of sender parameter. AnyObject

* func insertNewObject(sender: AnyObject) {

148

You don't need to do anything with that inside this function so let's have a look at tableView:cellForRowAtIndexPath: which will have an impact on you

* override func tableView(tableView: UITableView, cellForRowAtIndexPath indexPath: NSIndexPath) -> UITableViewCell {

* let cell = tableView.dequeueReusableCellWithIdentifier("Cell", forIndexPath: indexPath) as UITableViewCell

* let object = objects[indexPath.row] as NSDate

* cell.textLabel?.text = object.description

* return cell

* }

Notice on the first line of the function tableView:cellForRowAtIndexPath we have called dequeueeusableCellWithIdentifier:forIndexPath on the table view. This method's return type is AnyObject.

Any class may be returned by this specific function, therefore you'll have to type it applying the UITableViewCell that is visible near the bottom of the screen. In the future, you'll modify this to your custom-built cell of taskCell that you'll create in the future.

When using Cocoa frameworks it is normal due to the need to make them compatible with the old style of Objective C, where id is the return type. This is that it is a pointer towards any type of object. Keep in mind that Swift does not use of pointers everywhere it can, and that is the reason solutions like this were developed to make your code more secure.

The final aspect that is intriguing is that of the language used to marking comments. These work to allow you to divide and allow you to jump between the documents:

* // MARK Table View

If you utilize this syntax for comment, it is possible to split an entire file making it easier to move through it. This can also help readers know exactly what the function is related to each other in the file.

DetailViewController.swift

There is one more file we need to look at - the DetailViewController. It's a small file in comparison to the MasterViewController however, it has numerous excellent instances of the way Swift helps writers write more efficient code.

To start with, we have the @IBOutlet attribute, which is for the variable detailDescriptionLabel. In a similar way to how it was in the header files in Objective C, this particular variable attribute tells Interface Builder about this particular property on your DetailViewController:

* @IBOutlet weak var detailDescriptionLabel: UILabel!

It is possible that this variable was classified as weak since you don't want DetailViewController to control the view.

Then, there's the definition of a variable property which is at a fascinating. It has additional code to define the property's behavior which is directly beside its definition:

* var detailItem: AnyObject? {

* didSet{

* /* / / Update the view.

* self.configureView()

* }

* }

There's also an option to use AnyObject? Type, but the most fascinating element is the didSet's code block.

Properties are able to include sections of code that perform as a callback for the specific event. The most appealing aspect of this is that instead of defining a specific setter to execute this, you will be able to have a more precise understanding of what code is doing there.

The code clarifies that when detailItem has been established, at any time from now on, configureView will need become available. This is due to something related directly to the display has been changed. The callbacks are major significance to iOS applications, as a result of the expressiveness of code.

We have discussed optionals earlier we discussed briefly optionals since they are utilized frequently in iOS application development, and here's a second illustration of how to use these options.

* configurationView func() {* func configureView()

* /update the interface of the user for the item in detail.

* if let detail: AnyObject = self.detailItem {

* if let label = self.detailDescriptionLabel {

* label.text = detail.description

* }

* }

* }

Note that binding options are utilized within the IF statement. That means that if the assignment expression to the right side has some value and is transferred to the left during the length of the IF body. If that expression doesn't contain a value, the IF statement body is not considered. It's similar to how we check for null in Objective C however it's an easier and safer effective method of checking for nil.

What's Coming Next

In this portion of the tutorial, you did not actually wrote any code. Instead, you performed something that was more crucial. You thought about the way Swift influences the way we use our Cocoa Touch classes and API'sIn the absence of this you'd find yourself having to fight Swift when you attempt to write your applications in the same way you did in the past.

What you've accomplished is to learn how to build your application safer, and without having to use the expressiveness that is the Swift programming language. You can see clearly that Apple has put a lot of effort into the integration with the frameworks they have in place and ensured that they haven't missed any single detail.

After getting this part of the tutorial completed It's now time to begin creating your application.

Going back to the TaskMe application you built in the beginning using Xcode 6. We now must begin adding the real functionality.

Utilizing using the "TaskMe" application you created using Xcode 6. Now it's time to add some real-time features.

Your First Story

The first thing you'll be adding to your list is the capability to include a brand new project your list. After this feature is established, all you have to do is press"+" and type in the name of the task, along with the title of the task along with some notes if you wish it, and once you tap save, you will be able to go back to the task list.

Set up The Storyboard

We're trying to make it easy and straightforward for your users , so it is best that all they needed to do was hit the + button and have the new controller appear up. To begin with this, go to Main.storyboard.

You'll need two controllers in order to accomplish this:

* UINavigationController

* UIViewController

The latter will be embedded in the new UINavigationController (you will not be reusing the one that is already on your screen as that is for the main workflow. So, go to the bottom right hands side of the Xcode screen and drag out the UINavigationController and the UIViewController from the object library int the editor area.

Now delete the table view controller that UINavigationController created, hold down CTRL and click the UINavigationController. Drag it to the UIViewController it was created. A popup will pop up when you click on the root view controller under the relationship segue area. The UIViewController will now be embedded in the UINavigationController, ensuring that you will be able to add in Cancel and Save buttons later on.

Now it's time to set up a segue so that you can navigate to UINavigationController and UIViewController. Before you do, open the MasterViewController.swift file and delete these two lines from viewDidLoad:

*   let   addButton   = UIBarButtonItem(barButtonSystemItem: .Add, target: self, action: "insertNewObject:")

*   self.navigationItem.rightBarButtonItem   = addButton

After they've been removed, you can also erase InsertNewObject using the method.

Return to your Main. Storyboard file, and then go to the library of objects. Drag a Bar Button Item from the library to the right hand side of the navigation bar in MasterViewController. Go to the attributes inspector, and switch the identifier's name to add.

Now it's time to set up the segue from MasterViewController to UINavigationController. Press CTRL and drag from the new Bar Button Item that you created to the new UINavigationController. In the popup, navigate into the Action Segue section and choose Present Modally.

The new segue will look like a rectangle inside a circle and will be part of the arrow that goes between MasterViewController and UINavigationController. Make use of the Attributes Inspector in order to change the Identifier's setting to showAddTask

The final step is to set your screen. Go to the Object Library and drag out two text fields, putting them into UINavigationController. Place them in the way you would like to. Press CTRL and move the text fields as well as the view that contains them to establish the auto Layout restrictions.

Choose the primary Text Field; it's now time to make a little altering to the attributes in the

Inspector. The first step is to select the blank placeholder, and then edit it to include the Task Title. You can change the size of your font from 24 to using The font editor. You are able to access by clicking on the T icon just below the font.

Now , you'll want to be capable of playing around with the height and the width, so alter the Border style to the second option from the left. Now you can test with the height. You could making your text 60 points tall, and then set the alignment to be centered.

Then go next to the Text Field and do something similar. Perhaps make the text smaller maybe 16 points, make it smaller in height and maybe alter the text placeholder to read like Notes. The alignment should be to the left instead of center this time.

Go to the UINavigationController and click on the navigation bar. In the Attributes Inspector and alter the title to add Task. After this, you will already have 2 controllers and two fields. Next, you need to design the subclass of the UIViewController to be used on the new Screen for adding tasks.

Before doing that make sure you run the program, and you'll notice that you are able to access the new screen , but at this point you won't be able to return.

Creating the AddTaskViewController

Start in the menu File, then choose New, choose File. The shortcut to this is Cmd+N in the keyboard. This will let you begin creating the brand new AddTaskController file. If you're in iOSSource. Go to Options, then select Cocoa Touch Class. Select Next. There is an area that reads Subclass of UIViewController. Type in the name. Click on the Class field. At the end of the name include AddTask.

Make sure the checkbox to also create XIB files is not checked and Swift is chosen to be the preferred language. Select Next. Now you'll get a file dialog screen. Choose the location to which the file will go - probably the default option is the location you would like it to go to and then click Create.

Before you start editing the file you see be aware that you have to make this the class for the UIViewController which was created within the Storyboard. Go to Main. Storyboard, and select UIViewController that you created previously. Go into the Identity Inspector and set the class to AddTaskViewController. You can find the Identity Inspector in the panel on the left side of the screen It looks like the shape of a square and lines.

Now, your focus is on AddTaskViewController in the Interface Builder. Start your Agent Editor (the icon that appears in the toolbar resembles the look of a dress code) and you are now able to select the outlets that will are connected to your code and the Storyboard.

Hold down CTRL and drag from each Tet Field in turn to the top of the class definition for AddTaskViewController. Each field must be named according to, titleField and notesField. The result should be something that looks similar to this.

*   class   AddTaskViewController: UIViewController {

* @IBOutlet weak variable titleField: The UITextField!

* @IBOutlet weak var notesField: UITextField!

* override func viewDidLoad() {

If you've ever tried using Objective C to do any iOS work, you'll observe that this is like what you would see in those headers files.

@IBOutlet is a declaration the connection between your program as well as the Storyboard. It makes use of an implicitly wrapped optional, so that the set isn't required to start the controller for view. These can be set up as soon as the views are ready; in most cases, it won't even affect you because they will already be set by then, especially in viewDidLoad and viewWillAppear:animated.

The declaration of the variable is insufficient and the reason is to ensure that there aren't any references that aren't needed. Without this, the two UITextFields will be owned by AddTaskViewController and that means that the view will not be allowed to release when it wants to because the controller will be holding on to the subviews.

Cancellation of Task Creation

In the next step, you must create the Cancel button to ensure that your task doesn't save whenever you tap it. In lieu of saving it, the button will block the screen that created the task. Start the Main. Storyboard file and then drag the Bar Button Item from the Object Library. Put it on the left part of the navigation bar in the AddTaskViewController screen. Then, select the Bar Button item, then open the Attributes Inspector, and then change the Identifier's name to read Cancel.

You should make use of those standard version of UI elements due to two reasons that are accessibility and future security. It is possible to changed titles to Cancel but, suppose that in the near future, Apple changes cancel to read X for instance Your application will be fully prepared for that.

The standard elements have accessibility already built in and have been thoroughly examined by the best which Apple employs. Now, we must connect the Cancel button. You will have to design a new segue to Dismiss.

To open this file, click File and then click New to create an entirely new file. The dialog select iOS-Source- Cocoa Touch Class. Select Next, and then assign the Subclass of: UIStoryboardSegue. The class needs to be changed to DismissSegue. When you are in the Language dropdown menu, ensure that Swift is selected, not Objective C.

There's one more step to take before the class is able to be implemented in your Storyboard. It allows the Dismiss segue option to be displayed in the Interface builder. However, in the case of running time it will not work. This is due to something odd happening behind the scenes of Swift. This can be resolved by explicitly specifying Objective C's Objective Class name. After that the program will be able find the correct class. Therefore, you need to change the class's definition to make it appears like:

* @objc(DismissSegue) class DismissSegue: UIStoryboardSegue {

The declaration at the start - @objc(DismissSegue) This makes the class accessible to the Storyboard. As Swift grows, this might alter, but for the moment this is the only way to prevent your application from crash.

You must now make a procedure for the custom segue that will let you go away from the controller.

* override func perform() {

* if let controller = sourceViewController.presentingViewController ? {

* controller.dismissViewControllerAnimated(true, completion: nil)

* }

* }

After all that, you're ready to launch the application and witness all the hard work you put into motion.

The Task You've Been Working On

It is now time to gain something of value from this task - save it. To accomplish this, you'll need an option to save the task. Back to the Main.storyboard file, drag a Bar Button Item from the objects library and put it on the right side of the navigation bar in AddTaskViewController. Make sure it's selected, as well as the Attributes Inspector is opened is switched to save.

While you're within this folder, it's the perfect moment to get rid of some other thing. People who plan to use your app do not really care if the screen for list is actually an "Master" screen. For them, as far as it's concerned, it's an Task screen. So Double-click on Master to make it read Tasks. Now include a Dismiss Segue between Save and MasterViewController, in the same way you did earlier with Cancel.

If you wanted to start your application right now you should be able to select either option to remove the modal, if it's exactly what you're trying to accomplish. It would however be helpful to add tasks to the task list , and also to be able to have a Table View refresh to show the new task.

You must put these tasks in one place and you'll also require an understanding of the task's scope you can do not use the Save option and proceed to the next section.

It is crucial to define the business objects that you are primarily concerned with independently apart from your interface. This makes them more flexible and accessible, essential if wish to create an application compatible with every platform. There isn't much to be involved in this process to create an Task structure and an TaskStore class.

The task struct is created. Task structure

Open File and create a brand new file. You can also press Cmd+N. But this time it is not the time to create the Cocoa Touch Class; instead we're looking for an ordinary Swift file. Name the file Task It will automatically be added with .swift. The next step is to create an Task structure inside the file:

* struct Task{

* let title: String

* Let notes note: String

* init(title: String, notes: String) {

* self.title = title

* self.notes = notes

* }

* }

It is possible that you are thinking that there's no way to edit the file, and you're right. If you want to make it Mutable you'll go in the direction that Swift recommends you do and create an unchangeable value object.

If you need to alter an assignment then all you need to have to do is remove the previous one and replace it with a new one in the position. The application's users will perceive it as editing, however, from your standpoint the life of an engineer is easier.

The management of our TaskStore

The next step is to create a second Swift file to be used in the TaskStore. The TaskStore will be configured as a singleton, which allows users to access only one instance at any time you wish. This means you'll be in a position to add tasks or modify existing tasks in the amount you wish.

Now, you can create your Swift file the same way you did previously, however, this time name it TaskStore. TaskStore

```
* class TaskStore {* class TaskStore

* Class var sharedInstance TaskStore {•

* struct Static {* struct Static

• static Let instance is TaskStore()

* }

* Return Static.instance

* }

* var tasks: [Task] = []

* func add(task: Task) {

* tasks.append(task)

* }

* func replace(task atIndex: Task index: Int) {* func replace(task: Task; atIndex index: Int);

* tasks[index] = task

* }

* function get(index of the Int) {-> Task = Task

* return tasks[index]

* }

* }
```

The first few lines of this code are creating a way for you to use a singleton by giving you access with TaskStore.sharedInstance. There are some basic functions to get, add and remove tasks from the list.

Then later on you could, if desired, replace all of this with a more appropriate TaskStore class-based version which will be able to store every task across all launches, but this is sufficient for the purpose of this instruction.

Finalizing Your First Feature

And now, I've got an easy task for you. You must complete the Save feature you began earlier. There is no need to fret about displaying the list of tasks, since I will discuss it in the coming days. All you have to do is have the tasks saved to the TaskStore and I'll show the solution later!

A hint to help you - the trick is giving the segue that comes from the Save button a name and using the prepareForSegue:sender method.

What it should look like now

How did you fare with this problem? Like I said, this is the code you'd have to use to complete the challenge:

* if segue.identifier == "dismissAndSave" {

* Let Task = Task(title: titleField.text, notes: notesField.text)

* TaskStore.sharedInstance.add(task)

* }

It is also important to ensure you've set the correct identification set for each segue on the Storyboard.

We'll take in a moment to take some refresher on the things you've done until now. If you've followed this guide carefully and thoroughly, you'll have a good understanding about the improvements Swift makes to Apple frameworks and also about the way it's writing code. You've also begun your first feature , creating a task, which has been almost completed. Let's continue and finish this application.

Ending the Stopping

It's now time to finish off so open the Main.storyboard file again and ensure that the two segues that run between AddTaskViewController and MasterViewController have got good names. Perhaps something similar to dismissAndCancel or perhaps dismissAndSave. This will make sure that you will be able to identify these for your next steps.

Open AddTaskViewController.swift and set up the prepareForSegue:sender method:

* override func prepareForSegue(segue: UIStoryboardSegue, sender: AnyObject!) {

* if segue.identifier == "dismissAndSave" {

* Let the task be Task(title: titleField.text, notes: notesField.text)

* TaskStore.sharedInstance.add(task)

* }

* }

Make sure whether the segue you're making is actually the Save segues. If not, the Cancel segue already does exactly what you would like to accomplish that is nothing. It is best practice for every segue, regardless of whether it's the only one you're creating and to make it clear regarding the segue you're using the program for. So, if and the situation changes later on the programmer will be aware of the current state of affairs and how everything is connected.

Now is the time to assign an additional task to a continuous, making use of the two field text options to define the task. Then, you can use taskStore to ensure that the task is secure by placing it in the sharedInstance.

If you start the application at present all will be working until you are at the top of the list. There should be no money cash deposited and everything is running well at this point.

There is no point in saving the work when you aren't able to see it. So it's time to begin the second part.

There's no use in saving an action if you don't actually see it this is why it's time to begin exploring your next feature.

Listing the tasks to be completed

Before you start with the list of tasks, it is crucial to be aware that at this point there isn't any data being saved between launches. After you've completed this tutorial, you can go on and study CoreData. Also, you can explore Realm which is expected to be a simple alternative to CoreData.

Making Use of What You Already Have

Before you alter things to the max, let's look at what you can accomplish using what you have. In the beginning, when you first created the project you were provided with the MasterViewController which had all the methods for data source and delegate already configured for you as well as Deletion. You also have a basic DetailViewController.

Let's continue. Open up MasterViewController.swift so we can make some changes. The first thing we want to do is get rid of the objects property on the MasterViewController, because we don't need t. Delete the line that looks like this, at the top of the controller:

* Vari objects = NSMutableArray()

There is no need for that there any more, but in deleting it, you will cause code to be very upset. This property is utilized in many different locations, so you are able to explore the possibilities of correcting errors. Start at the top, and then replace the old code with the latest version which uses the TaskStore.

Open the Detail Screen

The first place you are going to see an error is in prepareForSegue:sender method that is in the MasterViewController. These changes must be made in this case, and they are to be made to the last two lines within the IF statement.

* override func prepareForSegue(segue: UIStoryboardSegue, sender: AnyObject?) {

```
* if segue.identifier == "showDetail" {

*       if    let     indexPath     =
self.tableView.indexPathForSelectedRow() {

*           let         task         =
TaskStore.sharedInstance.get(indexPath.row)

*       (segue.destinationViewController     as
DetailViewController).detailItem = task

* }

* }

* }
```

In the second line of the IF statement, you will need switch the value of the variable from object. To complete the task you require, utilize the Get method which is based on the sharedInstance of the TaskStore. There is no need to use casting since you are aware that you will receive an Task return from this method. Get method.

The third line of the IF statement the change is boring , really. All you have to do is change the detailItem in the DetailViewController's DetailViewController to task instead object. It is required because you've altered the name of the constant earlier.

172

Now you need to move on and fix a problem that has shown up elsewhere, namely in the DetailViewController so open the DetailViewControlle.swift file and make a minor change

No more any object

DetailViewController anticipates that there will exist an AnyObject? This means that an object won't work. It's easily fixable though simply by changing the of the detailItem's type to Task?

* var detailItem: Task? {

* didSet{

* / Make changes to the display.

* self.configureView()

* }

* }

While you're there, you can repair the rest of the controller. There's not much else to be done and all you have to do is change the configurationView method.

Take a look at the place the area where the optional detailItem is removed from the wrapper. In the moment you claim that it's AnyObject type, but that is no longer the case since you have changed the type. Therefore, it's time to fix it. Since Task doesn't have an attribute for description You need to change the t property to title

*   function   configureView()   {*   func configureView()

* /update the interface of the user for the item in detail.

* if let detail: Task = self.detailItem {

* if let label = self.detailDescriptionLabel {

* label.text = detail.title

* }

* }

* }

That is all you need to change in the DetailViewController, at least until there are some more design changes. Time to go back to MasterViewController.swift and finish off in there.

Change the Data Source, and Delegate

The next error that needs to be fixed is the UITableViewDataSource protocol method TableView:numberOfRowsInSection

In the moment, you're simply calling count on the object array. Instead, you'd like to call count using this shared instance in TaskStore

* override func tableView(tableView: UITableView, numberOfRowsInSection section: Int) -> Int {

* return TaskStore.sharedInstance.count

* }

You might be thinking about what you can do to accomplish this because you don't have a property count currently. Let's make one. Launch taskStore.swift and then, under the declaration of property for Tasks, insert this:

* {var count: Int Variant count: Int >

* get {

* return tasks.count

* }

* }

You could, if were interested, have designed it as a technique that is similar to this:

* Fic count() * func count() {* func count() -> Int

* return tasks.count

* }

Although that could be a better method however, it lacks some fashion. By turning Count to a property that is computed, you're keeping a consistent API Array. Don't try to force what is in essence an object into an algorithm - it will not be able to go.

What you might not realize is that you can be further than the definition of a method. If you are creating a computed property doesn't have an operator, which is why you could take lines 2 and 4 out and replace them with:

* {var count: Int Variant count: Int >

* return tasks.count

* }

This is so much better and more and expressive. It's clearly a property, and it is obvious the fact that this is a computation one. It is also evident the thing it is doing. Hello to Swift!

Return to the Source of the Data Source

We'll move past all the small details that are apparent in Swift and then finish our data sources. The tableView:numberOfRowsInSection: method is absolutely fine now so let's move on to tableView:cellForRowAtIndexPath method

176

The change here is somewhat similar to the change that you made to prepareForSegue:Sender method in the MasterViewController - all you are doing is changing how to get the task and the property that you are using it from

* override func tableView(tableView: UITableView, cellForRowAtIndexPath indexPath: NSIndexPath) -> UITableViewCell {

* let cell = tableView.dequeueReusableCellWithIdentifier(" Cell", forIndexPath: indexPath) as UITableViewCell

* let task = TaskStore.sharedInstance.get(indexPath.row)

* cell.textLabel?.text = task.title

* return cell

* }

These lines modified were the ones that appear right before the return statement. Now, you will make use of the get method in the TaskStore instead of the array of objects as well as its subscript operators. The result is assigned of an object variable to the task constant.

In the final line before the return clause, you've made a modification to the value you have set the text property of the textLabel to be alter it to the name of the task you were given using"the get" method.

One thing remains to be altered is the delegate method

Finalizing the Basics with the Delegate

It's likely that you've discovered that you only have only one option to alter. In the UITableViewDelegate method tableView:commitEditingStyle:forRowAtIndexP ath: you are going to make one simple change by adding in something to the TaskStore

* override func tableView(tableView: UITableView, commitEditingStyle editingStyle: UITableViewCellEditingStyle, forRowAtIndexPath indexPath: NSIndexPath) {

* If editingStyleis .Delete {the

*

TaskStore.sharedInstance.removeTaskAtIndex(i ndexPath.row)

*

tableView.deleteRowsAtIndexPaths([indexPath] , withRowAnimation: .Fade)

* else|} when editingStyle is .Insert {*

* brand new instance of the class you want to use add it to the array, and then add an additional row in the view of tables.

* }

* }

Another Method to Use TaskStore

Navigate to your TaskStore class and include the method to removeTaskAtIndex.

* func removeTaskAtIndex(index: Int) {

* tasks.removeAtIndex(index)

* }

The reason I've requested you to perform this instead of accessing directly the task array and then calling the removeAtIndex method , is because it allows you to create a custom API for customers of the TaskStore class. In the future, you'll be able to modify changes within the Internals TaskStore class without having to alter the other code.

Making Things a Little More Organized

There are a few small design tweaks you can do to improve the functionality of your application.

One of which is obvious design flaw: what do you think of the notes?

Modifying the Storyboard

Within the Main.storyboard file, choose the table view model cell. Then, switch in the cell from default UITableViewStyle using only one text label and change it to the style subtitle. This will allow you to see an overview of the notes. To accomplish this, open the Attributes Inspector, and then click Style. In the menu dropdown, choose Subtitle and you'll notice that the cell's prototype has changed and now has an additional label.

Making Updates to Your MasterViewController

Let's take advantage of that second label and make a few changes to MasterViewController. Open up the MasterViewController.swift file and locate the tableView:cellForRowAtIndexPath method. This is the method you are changing.

* override func tableView(tableView: UITableView, cellForRowAtIndexPath indexPath: NSIndexPath) -> UITableViewCell {

* let cell = tableView.dequeueReusableCellWithIdentifier("

Cell",   forIndexPath: indexPath)   as
UITableViewCell

*   let   task   =
TaskStore.sharedInstance.get(indexPath.row)

* cell.textLabel?.text = task.title

* cell.detailTextLabel?.text = task.notes

* return cell

* }

The only change that is significant here is setting the text property on the detailTextLabel. The text property will be set between the property text of textLabel as well as the line that the cell returns from the method.

Try the application out and then try adding an item to the list. Make sure you fill out the notes section. You'll see an overview of the notes once the task list appears. Don't overfill the notes. If you have too much to fit onto the detailTextLabel the text will be cut off, which is the next task to solve.

The Design View is being redesigned Detail View

That small label in the center really isn't going to be enough so open up Mail.storyboard.swift and get ready to make some changes to

DetailViewController. It isn't really a matter of how you modify this to alter the way it appears, as long as you've got the correct two views. The fit is already apparent in DetailViewController. All you have change is to move it upwards to make it look a more large, but don't forget to modify the constraints.

The next thing to do is drag a Tet View out of the Objects Library to the DetailViewController. After the layout has been sorted out, you are able to go to the Attributes Inspector and make changes.

The font is able to be expanded to 18 pointsusing the font picker. This should be a familiar feature. It is accessible via the T icon right next on the type. Make sure to uncheck the box beside Editable You will see it right beneath the field for the font. Another thing that is nice would be that you could access the phone numbers and links from the notes section. So when you are in the Detection section within Attributes Inspector, ensure that you check the boxes to include Phone numbers and Links.

Lastly, you should link the Text View and the DetailedViewController. Start The Assistant Editor (remember that it's the icon which looks like an elegant suit) and press CTRL. Drag the

Text View to the point where you've identified the @IBOutlet that will be used for the detailTextLabel. The new outlet will be called notesView.

Highlighting Your Notes

Once the outlet is created the only thing left is placing the content. Open DetailViewController.swift and locate configureView method. Change these settings:

* configurationView func() {* func configureView()

* /update your user interface to reflect the item in detail.

* if let detail: Task = self.detailItem {

* if let label = self.detailDescriptionLabel {

* label.text = detail.title

* }

* }

* }

The modifications are in the IF statement that is located inside the wrap IF statement. Also, you have removed the useless use of self which was at the front of all the properties.

The first step is to remove the optional UITextView even though it's been wrapped. It must then assign to the variable named notes, which allows you to use noteView's text property as an item's notes attribute of the details item which is a task.

When you launch the application , you'll be able to be presented with a simple task management application that you can explore to your heart's content.

Congratulations! You've successfully created an entirely new iOS app using Swift. Although it's unlikely to be the next huge thing, it's an excellent starting point to learn from, and begin to understand the basics of using Swift as well as Xcode to create an application. If you built similar apps using Objective C, you'd be able to have a lot more code than the one you've seen in this program and, perhaps even more importantly there would be a lot less explicit code.

www.ingramcontent.com/pod-product-compliance
Lightning Source LLC
Chambersburg PA
CBHW071121050326
40690CB00008B/1294